Job Interview Tips for People
With Not-So-Hot Backgrounds

D1004814

By Ron & Caryl Krannich, Ph.Ds

CAREER AND BUSINESS BOOKS AND SOFTWARE

101 Dynamite Answers to Interview Questions
101 Secrets of Highly Effective Speakers
201 Dynamite Job Search Letters
America's Top 100 Jobs for People Without a Four-Year Degree
America's Top Internet Job Sites
Best Jobs for the 21st Century
Change Your Job, Change Your Life
The Complete Guide to Public Employment
The Directory of Federal Jobs and Employers
Discover the Best Jobs for You!
Dynamite Cover Letters
Dynamite Networking for Dynamite Jobs
Dynamite Resumes
Dynamite Salary Negotiations
Dynamite Tele-Search
The Educator's Guide to Alternative Jobs and Careers
Find a Federal Job Fast!
From Air Force Blue to Corporate Gray
From Army Green to Corporate Gray
From Navy Blue to Corporate Gray
Get a Raise in 7 Days
High Impact Resumes and Letters
I Want to Do Something Else, But I'm Not Sure What It Is
Interview for Success
Job Hunting Guide
Job Interview Tips for People With Not-So-Hot Backgrounds
Job Power Source and *Ultimate Job Source* (software)
Jobs and Careers With Nonprofit Organizations
Military Resumes and Cover Letters
Moving Out of Education
Moving Out of Government
Nail the Job Interview!
No One Will Hire Me!
Re-Careering in Turbulent Times
Resumes & Job Search Letters for Transitioning Military Personnel
Savvy Interviewing
Savvy Networker
Savvy Resume Writer

TRAVEL AND INTERNATIONAL BOOKS

Best Resumes and CVs for International Jobs
The Complete Guide to International Jobs and Careers
Directory of Websites for International Jobs
International Jobs Directory
Jobs for Travel Lovers
Mayors and Managers in Thailand
Politics of Family Planning Policy in Thailand
Shopping and Traveling in Exotic Asia
Shopping in Exotic Places
Shopping in the Exotic South Pacific
Travel Planning on the Internet
Treasures and Pleasures of Australia
Treasures and Pleasures of China
Treasures and Pleasures of Egypt
Treasures and Pleasures of Hong Kong
Treasures and Pleasures of India
Treasures and Pleasures of Indonesia
Treasures and Pleasures of Italy
Treasures and Pleasures of Mexico
Treasures and Pleasures of Morocco and Tunisia
Treasures and Pleasures of Paris and the French Riviera
Treasures and Pleasures of Rio and São Paulo
Treasures and Pleasures of Santa Fe, Taos, and Albuquerque
Treasures and Pleasures of Singapore and Bali
Treasures and Pleasures of Singapore and Malaysia
Treasures and Pleasures of Southern Africa
Treasures and Pleasures of Thailand and Myanmar
Treasures and Pleasures of Turkey
Treasures and Pleasures of Vietnam and Cambodia

Job Interview Tips
for People With Not-So-Hot Backgrounds
—— *How to Put Red Flags Behind You to Win the Job* ——

Caryl Rae Krannich, Ph.D.
Ronald L. Krannich, Ph.D.

IMPACT PUBLICATIONS
Manassas Park, Virginia

Job Interview Tips for People With Not-So-Hot Backgrounds

ISBN: 1-57023-213-X

Library of Congress: 2004100257

Publisher: For information on Impact Publications, including current and forthcoming publications, authors, press kits, online bookstore, and submission requirements, visit the left navigation bar on the front page of our main company website: www.impactpublications.com.

Publicity/Rights: For information on publicity, author interviews, and subsidiary rights, contact the Media Relations Department: Tel. 703-361-7300, Fax 703-335-9486, or email: info@impactpublications.com.

Sales/Distribution: All bookstore sales are handled through Impact's trade distributor: National Book Network, 15200 NBN Way, Blue Ridge Summit, PA 17214, Tel. 1-800-462-6420. All special sales and distribution inquiries should be directed to the publisher: Sales Department, IMPACT PUBLICATIONS, 9104 Manassas Drive, Suite N, Manassas Park, VA 20111-5211, Tel. 703-361-7300, Fax 703-335-9486, or email: info@impactpublications.com.

Contents

Preface .... **ix**

**1 What Employers Want in
Today's Job Market** **1**

- Fictitious Backgrounds, Cautious Employers   2
- The Truth About You   3
- Positive Workplace Characteristics   4
- Predicting Your Best Behavior   5
- Employee Who Shows Up for Work   5
- Employee Who Gets Along With Co-Workers   6
- Employee Who Follows Orders   7
- Employee Who Listens to Instructions   8
- Employee Who Is Trustworthy   9
- Employee Who Will Stay With the Company   9
- Employers Want the Truth About You   11
- Think Like the Employer   11

2 People With Not-So-Hot Backgrounds **13**

- Red Flag Days   14
- Risky Business   16
- No Experience   17
- Poor Grades   17
- No Diploma or Degree   17

- Been Fired   18
- Job Hopper   18
- No Focus to the Jobs Held   19
- Poor References   19
- Criminal Record   20
- Over-Qualified   20
- Test Your Knock-Out Potential   21
- Identify and Deal With Your Red Flags   22

3 Clues Employers Look for to Determine Successful "Fit" 24

- Looking for Hiring Clues   25
- Verbal Exchange   25
- Nonverbal Cues   26
- Comparing Verbal and Nonverbal Messages   27
- Appearance and Dress   27
- Tone of Voice and Eye Contact   28
- Gestures   28
- Facial Expression   28
- Body Language   29
- What's Your True Message?   29
- Ask Yourself   30

4 Turn Red Flags Into Green Lights 32

- Identify Your Personal Red Flags   33
- Questions That Follow Red Flags   38
- Prepare to Lower Your Red Flags   39
- Get Rid of the Red Flag(s)   42
- Plan the Gist of Your Explanations   43

5 Prepare to Meet the Employer's Needs: The Verbal Exchange 45

- Research the Company and the Job   46
- Match Your Goals/Strengths to the Employer's Needs   47
- Prepare to Complete an Application or Test   48
- Prepare for Questions   50
- Questions About Your Personal Life   51
- Questions About Your Education   52

- Questions About Your Experience   52
- Questions About Your Accomplishments and
  Work Style   52
- Questions About Your Goals and Motivation   53
- Questions About Your Future Goals/Plans   54
- Practice for the Interview   54
- Ask Yourself   55

6 Nonverbal Behaviors That Meet
Needs and Exceed Expectations 56

- Manage Your Physical Appearance
  and Dress – Men   57
- Manage Your Physical Appearance and
  Dress – Women   58
- Make Your Body Language Say Positive Things
  About You   59
- Eye Contact and Facial Expression   61
- Vocal Expression   62
- Your Total Nonverbal Message   62
- Ask Yourself   63

7 At the Interview: Wow the Interviewer 64

- Good Preparation Wins   65
- Last Minute Advice   65
- Entering the Office and Waiting for the Interviewer   67
- As the Interview Begins   68
- During the Interview   76
- Listen for Underlying Messages and Questions   69
- Dealing With Questions About a Difficult
  Background   71
- Accentuate the Positive   72
- Ask Yourself   73

8 Avoid 35 Common Interview Errors 74

- It's a Very Stressful Time   75
- Mistakes You Shouldn't Make   75

9 Challenging Questions and Sample Answers 85

- 101 Questions You May Be Asked   86
- Unexpected and Wacky Questions   91
- Behavior- and Situation-Based Questions   93
- Red Flag Questions and Issues   94
  - Poor Grades   95
  - No Diploma   97
  - Were Fired   98
  - Job Hopper   100
  - No Focus to Jobs Held   102
  - Poor References   103
  - Ex-Offender   105
  - Abused Drugs or Alcohol   109
  - Over-Qualified   110
- Questions You Should Ask   111
- Ask Yourself   112

10 Close and Follow Up the Interview 114

- Respond to a Job Offer   115
- Close With No Job Offer . . . Yet   116
- Send a Thank You Letter   117
- Ask Yourself   119

11 When You Need Help Along the Way 120

- Alternative Career Services   121
- Locating a Certified Career Professional   128
- Dealing With Difficult Backgrounds   128
- Useful Books and Websites   129
- Ask Yourself   131

Index 133

The Authors 137

Career Resources 139

Preface

MOST INTERVIEW BOOKS are designed with an ideal job seeker in mind – a candidate who is well educated, credentialed, goal-oriented, skilled, and accomplished. Pick up almost any resume book and you'll see many examples of perfect candidates who seem to do everything right in their education and work lives. Examine a few job interview books and you'll see examples of interviewees who often stretch the imagination, because they seem so well qualified and successful.

Unfortunately, most job seekers do not fit this model of success and thus few of them can relate to such examples. In fact, front-line career professionals seldom encounter such ideal candidates. Instead, they are more likely to work with people who have not-so-hot backgrounds. Many such job seekers have made poor choices, experienced bad luck, and are in need of professional help to turn their lives around. For them, life is already tough enough and then they have to get and keep a job!

We wrote this book because we saw a pressing need to break out of the "successful job search candidate" box and address a major issue affecting millions of not-so-successful job seekers today – what to do about a not-so-hot background that includes red flags or potential job knock-out issues. Consider these basic facts of life in America:

- Over 20 million people lose their jobs each year.
- Over 600,000 ex-offenders are released into communities each year.
- Over 2 million people are currently incarcerated.
- Over 5 million people are on parole or probation.
- Over 30 million people have been convicted of a crime.
- Over 15 million workers lack a high school diploma or equivalent.

Millions of other people have difficulty keeping a job, change jobs frequently, lack appropriate workplace skills, and/or generate poor references.

This is often the "forgotten" and most challenging segment of America's workforce. Many of these people have difficult or not-so-hot backgrounds that relegate them to the lower end of the labor market and economy – low paying and unstable jobs with little or no career future. They appear unemployable because they lack strong employability skills and exhibit weak work habits. Employers all too often regard these individuals as more trouble than they are worth. Employers interpret red flags in people's backgrounds as signs of potentially difficult hires – they come to the workplace with a troubled history and an unattractive pattern of behavior employers would rather avoid. These are often the people local government employment programs, such as Workforce Development, and nonprofit social service organizations, such as Goodwill Industries, work with as they try to help them create a new and more employable life. It involves millions of people in communities across the country, from New York City, Baltimore, Atlanta, and Miami to Peoria, Kansas City, Albuquerque, Los Angeles, and Portland.

As we note throughout this book, employers want what they have always wanted in employees – truthfulness, character, and value. They also are forgiving of mistakes as long as individuals are willing to take responsibility and can demonstrate sincere efforts to change their behavior for the better. Such changes take place through new attitudes, goal setting, education, training, and counseling. Indeed, we live in a culture where forgiveness, redemption, and self-transformation are highly valued and rewarded.

> *Employers want what they have always wanted in employees – truthfulness, character, and value.*

As you will quickly discover in our examples, this is not a book about how people with not-so-hot backgrounds can develop clever interview skills to con employers into hiring them. Rather, it's a book about how people with difficult backgrounds need to first change their lives by becoming more employable. It begins with changes in attitudes and motivations related to a purpose in life. Our candidates communicate these changes to employers who become forgiving of red flag behaviors and who conclude they are most likely hiring someone who gives them truthfulness, character, and value. In other words, the prerequisite for making this book work is self-transformation.

This book builds on our earlier effort in **No One Will Hire Me! Avoid 15 Mistakes and Win the Job** (Impact Publications, 2004) to address several key job search issues and mistakes that lead to job search failure. **Job Interview Tips for People With Not-So-Hot Backgrounds** goes one step further in primarily focusing on the critical job interview for people with difficult backgrounds. Taken together these two books cover all the basics for conducting an effective job search.

Three terms appear interchangeably throughout this book. We use "he" as a gender-neutral term. When we refer to "he," we also mean "she," and vice versa. The term "company" is an all-inclusive term. When we refer to "company," we also mean "organization," which could include nonprofit organizations, trade and professional associations, and government agencies rather than just businesses. "Employer" and "interviewer" also are used interchangeably.

If you have red flags in your background, make sure they are not continuing impediments to your employability. Begin thinking like the employer by focusing on what is really valued in today's workplace. Make the necessary changes in your behavior and communicate those changes in the critical job interview. If you can do that, you may open yourself to a whole new world of satisfying and rewarding work.

Ron and Caryl Krannich
krannich@impactpublications.com

Job Interview Tips for People With Not-So-Hot Backgrounds

1

What Employers Want in Today's Job Market

E MPLOYERS TODAY WANT what they have always wanted from their employees – **truthfulness, character, and value**. But they are more apprehensive than ever when screening candidates for positions. What they initially see – on the resume or application or in job interviews – is not what they often get once they hire the individual. They want to better predict your future performance based on a clear understanding of your background and patterns of behavior.

Fictitious Backgrounds, Cautious Employers

Recent research indicates nearly two-thirds of all job seekers intentionally or unintentionally include inaccurate information on their applications and resumes, from details about their education background (fictitious degrees, schools, and accomplishments) and criminal background (over 30 million U.S. citizens have a conviction record with over 5 million having a history of incarceration) to employers, employment dates, positions, responsibilities, and awards. Many simply lie about who they are and what they can do in order to get the job. They cover up not-so-hot backgrounds with positive tales they think will impress employers. These inaccuracies often spill over into the job interview with disingenuous and deceptive answers to questions.

> *Employers want to better predict your performance based on an understanding of your background and patterns of behavior.*

Employers increasingly do four things in order to compensate for possible inaccurate or incomplete information received from candidates:

1. **Conduct background checks of candidates** in order to verify credentials, uncover any red flag behaviors (see Chapter 2) that could be detrimental to the company, and provide a complete personal and professional profile of the candidate. Background checks come in many different forms – speaking with candidate-supplied references, contacting previous employers, and using an independent background investigation firm that may cover many sensitive issues that cannot be legally addressed during a job interview – criminal background, marital status, family his-

tory, credit history, health issues, insurance claims, legal suits, etc.

2. **Ask more probing behavior-based questions during job interviews.** Unlike standard *who, what, where,* and *when* interview questions, behavior-based questions (see Chapter 9) are more difficult to prepare for, and responses to such questions are more revealing of a candidate's true motivations, character, patterns of behavior, and decision-making style. They require candidates to give examples of their performance as well as address hypothetical *"What if . . ."* situations.

3. **Subject candidates to multiple job interviews.** Some candidates may be called back for five or six interviews. Multiple job interviews give employers a chance to throughly examine a candidate and observe any inconsistencies from one interview to another.

4. **Administer a variety of revealing tests**, from aptitude tests and drug exams to personality profiles and psychological tests, during the job interview. Some companies dealing with sensitive security issues may require a polygraph examination as a pre-condition for employment. These instruments give employers additional information for assessing the qualifications, veracity, and "fit" of candidates.

The Truth About You

Beginning on their application or resume and proceeding through the job interview, many candidates are less than truthful about their backgrounds, motivations, and performance. Many exaggerate their accomplishments, cover up problems with their personality and work behavior, and present an inaccurate picture of their performance. Some deliberately con employers by lying or being deceptive in order to get the job. It's only after they have worked with the new employee for a few weeks that employers learn the truth about what they have really acquired – a difficult hire who presents more problems than he or she is worth. Understandably, employers are suspicious of candidates because of previous negative experiences with employees.

Positive Workplace Characteristics

Employers try to avoid hiring mistakes by looking for people who combine many of these positive personality and workplace characteristics:

- Dependable
- Cooperative
- Attentive
- Focused
- Purposeful
- Loyal
- Predictable
- Talented
- Enthusiastic
- Trustworthy
- Intelligent
- Positive
- Problem-solver
- Conscientious
- Motivated
- Reliable
- Resourceful
- Responsible
- Literate
- Articulate

- Discreet
- Flexible
- Sensitive
- Honest
- Sincere
- Effective
- Efficient
- Precise
- Diligent
- Versatile
- Perceptive
- Tactful
- Astute
- Patient
- Tenacious
- Receptive
- Organized
- Adaptive
- Successful

Of course employers want to hire someone who has the skills to do the job, but even if you can do the job, the further question is *"Will you?"* How motivated are you to do the job well from one day to another? Can you deliver quality performance? These and many other important questions are on the minds of employers who make screening and hiring decisions. They are questions you need to address as you prepare for the all-important job interview.

Predicting Your Best Behavior

Employers increasingly acknowledge their need to hire smarter – find people who have a background of consistent, dependable, and competent performance. Before hiring you, they want to predict your future performance based on an understanding of your past patterns of behavior. If you approach an employer with a not-so-hot background, you'll need to convince him or her that you will both meet and exceed the expectations for the job in question.

"Will you do the job I hire you to do?" is a different question than *"Can you do the job?"* The first question deals with motivation while the second question deals with skills. Another question on the employer's mind is, *"Will you be dependable?"* Even if you can do the job, but you don't show up for work much of the time when you are scheduled to work, the fact that you can do the job isn't worth very much. If you aren't there to do your work, you do not provide value to the employer.

Employee That Shows Up for Work

Many employers can relate to the old adage that *"showing up is half the job."* After all, they often encounter employees who don't regularly come to work or they keep unpredictable hours. Being dependable by coming to work regularly and on time is one of the most important expectations of employers. Failure to meet this expectation is grounds for being fired.

A publisher we know had an employee whose job was in the warehouse. Mary checked in books that came into the warehouse from other publishers and she pulled the books and packed books to be shipped out to clients who had placed orders for them. She did a great job *when* she showed up for work. She was one of the fastest workers the company had and her error rate was one of the lowest. In other words, she rarely shipped the wrong book by mistake. Ideal employee? She could have been. But her attendance record was terrible. The employer never knew whether she would show up for work or not. Much of her absent time was ostensibly because of illness. But whether her reasons for missing work were legitimate or not made little difference to the employer. The bottom line was the company's performance – work was not getting done, and the employer could not depend on her to be at work the next day either. So with reluctance, the employer had to let the employee go. Even though she could do the work, and did do the work in an exemplary fashion when she showed up for work, she was fired because her long-term work pattern was one of undependability. The employer could not depend on her to be there to get the work accomplished.

> *Employers expect dependability in their employees.*

Employee Who Gets Along With Co-Workers

Employers want to hire a worker who will get along well with others. They want someone who will fit within the organization and not be a trouble maker or burden. So interpersonal skills are an important consideration in making a hiring decision. Simply doing the work is not enough if the new hire creates more problems in the process.

It wasn't until John was on the job for five months that his boss and co-workers noticed a significant change in his behavior – he had what appeared to be a serious anger problem. This was totally unexpected since John was such a wonderful team player who seemed to get along with everyone. This perceived anger problem manifested itself on the job in several ways: John talked a lot, usually in conspiratory language, about his problems with his neighbors; he often got in arguments with co-workers; he seemed to have a fascination with guns; and he was sometimes abusive to customers. He seldom had a positive thing to say about anyone, including his family. He even threatened a co-worker who told him to "cool it." Not surprising, most co-workers avoided working with John because of his volatile temper. In fact, many of his co-workers felt uncomfortable working around him. Some suspected he had a bipolar disorder because of his frequent mood swings. His boss spoke to him about his so-called anger problem and, indeed, learned John was bipolar. He also learned that John was properly diagnosed and was supposed to treat his disorder with medication. However, he was not following the prescribed regimen for fear of gaining

> *Interpersonal skills are an important consideration in making a hiring decision. Simply doing the work is not enough.*

weight. His recent problems were related to his failure to take the medication. John was given notice that he had to get back to his "normal self" or he would be dismissed. His behavior had severely disrupted the workplace, with many co-workers fearing for their safety. Some even began coming to work with mace – just in case John became violent! This meeting literally became John's "wake-up call" to get his life and career back on track. He's back on his drug regimen and continues to be a productive worker. His co-workers are amazed at the positive changes in John's behavior. John has even gone so far as to explain his health situation to several co-workers. Understanding his situation, they are very supportive of him and genuinely enjoy working with him – as long as he stays on his medication!

Employee Who Follows Orders

Employers want to hire an individual who is willing to follow orders or directions given by the boss or supervisor(s) as well as work in a team environment. They do not want to hire someone who rebels against authority, won't follow orders, or can't work with teams.

Jason liked to play the "Lone Ranger" – set and achieve his own goals. He often rebelled against authority, which seemed to show on his resume. Indeed, he appeared to be a job-hopper – five different employers in eight years. When asked during the interview about his frequent job changes, he seemed to be disingenuous – "*Advancing my career.*" However, the job moves did not appear to indicate much career advancement – only different jobs. Chances are he was fired from several of these jobs. When asked to give an example of how he solved problems as a team member, he couldn't give a good example of such an experience. When asked about his management philosophy, he didn't seem to understand the concepts of supervision and accountability. Indeed, he shifted the discussion to examples of his own achievements and asked about salary and benefits. His language focused on "me" rather than "us." Since the job in question required strong team-building skills and close supervision and accountability, Jason was not called back for a second interview. Despite Jason's extensive experience, the employer felt his work style was not appropriate for this company's work culture. In re-reading his resume, the employer felt he made a mistake by not carefully reading between the lines – five jobs in eight years with little career advancement should have indicated a potential employability problem.

Employee Who Listens to Instructions

Employers want to hire an individual who will listen to instructions and be willing to learn how things are expected to be done at their company rather than a someone who wants to do things the way they were done at a former organization the new employee worked for.

Marlene was well prepared for the job interview. She practiced giving answers to nearly 100 hypothetical questions she might be asked at the job interview. Unfortunately, she arrived 15 minutes late for the interview and gave a killer excuse – the employer's directions were not very clear and consequently she got lost. Throughout the interview she seemed anxious to give her prepared answers to questions. The only problem was that the employer asked a few behavior-based questions she was unprepared for! For example:

"*Give me an example of how you followed the advice of your boss despite your better judgment.*"

"*Give me an example of how you solved a customer's billing problem.*"

"How would you deal with a customer who complained about the poor service she received from our company?"

"What would you do if I told you to take the trash out and you felt that was not in your job description?"

"What problems are you prepared to solve in our company? How would you go about solving them?"

Marlene was not offered the job because she didn't handle these questions well. She either wasn't listening or failed to give thoughtful answers reflecting her willingness to learn.

Employee Who is Trustworthy

Employers want to hire an individual they can trust. They want someone whom they can trust not to steal from them or other employees; trust not to "fudge" the hours worked on a time card; trust not to use alcohol or illegal substances in the workplace; trust not to share "privileged information" (company secrets) with people outside the company.

Detrick couldn't be trusted for several reasons. Not only did he frequently miss work, when he did come to work he goofed off about 30 percent of the time and made numerous errors. He sometimes came to work with alcohol on his breath and constantly received phone calls from his seemingly upset girl friend. Some of his equipment mysteriously vanished and his supplies seemed to be quickly depleted. He soon become more trouble than he was worth. After repeated warnings about this behavior, Detrick was fired.

Employee Who Will Stay With the Company

Although employers today don't expect a new employee to commit a lifetime to the job or the company, employers do want to hire people who will stay with the company for a while. Hiring and training new employees costs a lot of money, and a rapid turnover of employees drains the company's profit potential.

Yvonne was invited to a job interview because of her impressive resume which included experience, skills, and accomplishments directly related to a home security position. However, she had one potential red flag in her background that needed clarification. In rereading and analyzing her resume, the employer was concerned that Yvonne had held five jobs in the past three years in two different career fields. Did she lack focus, encounter problems on the job, or did she have a case of job wanderlust – constantly looking for a new job? Since the company spent a great deal of time and money training its personnel, it was important that employees stay with the company for at least three years. Her history of frequent employment changes would be a central concern during the interview. Yvonne seemed to do everything right at the initial stages of the interview – dressed well, good eye contact, and very personable. She did well with small talk and seem to be very bright and enthusiastic. However, she started having trouble answering several questions relating to her employment history. For example, when asked about her goals and what she hoped to be

What Employers Want From You

- You have the skills to do the job
- You are dependable
- You will fit into the organization:
  - You can get along with co-workers
  - You can get along with bosses
- You will follow orders (instructions) given by your boss(es)
- You will listen and be able/willing to learn new things and new ways of doing things
- You can be trusted
- If hired, you will stay with the company for a while

doing five years from now, Yvonne stumbled. Her goals tended to be personal – new home and marriage – and her five-year plan seemed disingenuous – in a management position within this company. When it came time to explain what she liked and disliked about her previous jobs, she again turned to personal concerns – salary and benefits. She seemed to lack any professional goals or a sense of how a career should advance over a five-year period. Her most revealing comment arose within five minutes of starting the interview – she asked about salary, health benefits, and vacation days! When praised for her impressive resume, she said she learned a great deal working with a professional resume writer. Then she talked on and on about her difficult life and the types of people she disliked working around. She volunteered another nugget of information – she had never been fired from these jobs since she left on her own for "better opportunities." Within 15 minutes of beginning the interview, the employer knew Yvonne would not be a good "fit" for the job. In the end, it appeared she just needed another job to pay her bills. She would most likely quit this job within a few months, especially after learning it required a serious commitment of time and effort to building a career within this company. While Yvonne seemed to have great job-related skills, her self-centered motivations and attitudes would not sustain her long within this company. Indeed, she would most likely continue on her path of job wanderlust as she accumulated more experience burning through many more employers.

Employers Want the Truth About You

Employers are apprehensive that even if they successfully identify an individual with the skills to do the job, they may make a mistake in hiring because the new employee may be lacking in one or more of the other areas of concern. Why are they afraid of making a bad hiring decision? Because it has happened to them before! The person who looked so good on paper (the resume) that he was invited to the interview and who demonstrated during the interview that he had the skills to do the job was a disaster after he was hired. One employee who did do good work when he showed up, didn't show up for work at all much of the time. Another employee couldn't get along with the other workers or with the boss. Yet another employee stole things from the work site. In each case the employer had no choice but to fire the employee and start the hiring process all over again and it cost both time and money. Now this employer is angry and scared. He is angry at the employee he had to fire for conning him; he is angry at himself for letting himself be conned; and he is afraid it will happen again with another potential employee.

Think Like the Employer

Consider the following situations/questions to determine your understanding of the employer's point of view and the dilemma the employer faces.

1. If a candidate for a job has the skills to do the job, why should the employer worry about anything else?

2. What are three other things, in addition to the skills to do the job, the employer wants in an employee? (There are at least six.)

3. Why does the employer care whether I stay with the company for only a few weeks or months?

4. When is an employer likely to be suspicious of my motives (think I may be conning him) when I go for a job interview?

5. What positive workplace characteristics (see pages 4-5) can I truthfully communicate to employers?

2

People With Not-So-Hot Backgrounds

W HEN PEOPLE ARE LOOKING for a job, a difficult or not-so-hot background is something in their past that raises a red flag in the employer's/interviewer's mind. Such red flags can become job knock-outs since they may indicate a lack of competence, a history of work problems, a lack of goals and focus, personality problems, interpersonal difficulties, unstable work habits, or being fired or incarcerated for valid on-the-job reasons. They reveal potential hiring problems employers would rather avoid.

If you have such red flags in your background, you need to do something about them before employers discover them on your resume, in a job interview, or on the job.

> *Employers look for clues that tell them not to hire you - your* **red flag** *behaviors.*

Always keep in mind that employers are looking for reasons to both hire you and not hire you. They look for positive signs that tell them you are the right person for the job. At the same time, they are searching for clues that tell them not to hire you. Being naturally suspicious of candidates who often put on a positive face to get the job, they are especially sensitive to any negative signs that tell them you are a potential problem employee. These negative signs are what we call **red flags**.

Red Flag Days

Employers are looking for individuals who have a positive **predictable pattern of performance**. Focusing on company goals, ideally they want to hire people with very promising backgrounds – self-starters and team players who can quickly achieve results for the company or organization. While they often settle for less and even operate employee assistance programs for people experiencing difficulties – from drug and alcohol abuse programs to mental health counseling – employers prefer to hire employees who do not need help dealing with their personal and/or professional problems. They shy away from hiring anyone who appears to have a difficult background requiring special on-the-job assistance. In other words, they don't want to hire or inherit your personal or job-related problems.

Many instant red flags often relate to health, legal, financial, personal, learning, and behavioral problems in your past, especially on previous jobs. Some of the most common such problems include:

- History of arrests and/or incarceration
- Chronic health problems, especially mental (bipolar disorder, schizophrenia, depression, etc.)
- Drug or alcohol abuse
- Learning disorder (slow learner, ADD, or ADHD)
- Physical handicap
- Abusive personality
- Violent behavior
- Lack of honesty and integrity
- Bankruptcy or heavily indebted
- Family difficulties (divorce, child custody, child care, elder care, finances, spouse, parents, significant other)

While some of these problems are protected by the Americans for Disabilities Act (ADA) or they are illegal for employers to actually ask candidates about, nonetheless, they raise serious hiring issues with employers who must still deal with these issues when making hiring decisions. Whether they are revealed in your application and/or resume, in an interview, by references, or through a background check, be prepared to address these potential knock-out issues with positive stories and responses.

> *Be prepared to address potential knock-out issues with positive stories and responses.*

If you have ever been fired for the following high-risk behaviors, you have red flags in your background which may knock you out of consideration for a job should the employer learn about them from you, your references, or a background check:

High-Risk Firing Behaviors

- Absent and tardy
- Bad attitude
- Broke rules
- Dishonest
- Insubordinate
- Incompetent

- Lying
- Stealing
- Unpredictable behavior
- Uncooperative
- Drug or alcohol abuse

- Abuse co-workers and/or clients
- Fighting on the job
- Lazy and slothful
- Undependable

Risky Business

Interviewing, selecting, and hiring a new employee is risky business. The employer has no doubt made some poor hiring decisions in the past and wants to avoid making another costly mistake. The employer knows that some job applicants will stretch the truth and some will even blatantly lie about their past to cover up problems that might knock them out of consideration for the job. So most interviewers find it easier to look for reasons **not** to hire a job seeker than to focus on identifying reasons why that person should be hired. Employers assume a person's past behaviors are the best predictors they have of the applicant's future patterns of behavior.

> *If any one knock-out objection is uncovered, the interviewer may view this as an indication the applicant should not be hired.*

Thus, if any one knock-out objection is uncovered, the interviewer may view this as an indication the applicant should not be hired. If there are more than one knock-out objection in the applicant's background, there is a lot the candidate has to overcome to be given serious consideration for the job. We will look at possible strategies to overcome knock-out objections in Chapter 4, deal with specific knock-out issues in a question/answer format in Chapter 8, and direct you toward professional assistance in Chapter 10.

Let's examine several of the most common knock-out objections employers hold.

No Experience

Having no experience puts one in the age-old chicken/egg dilemma. You can't get a job if you don't have experience; yet you can't gain experience if you can't get a job. Experience is not necessary for many entry-level jobs or jobs requiring few specialized skills, such as stocking shelves in a store or bagging groceries at the check-out counter. But for many jobs employers do prefer or even require experience, or an applicant will not even be considered for the job. Employers prefer job candidates who have experience either doing the job they are interviewing for or a job that uses very similar skills, because they see it as an indicator the applicant has the ability to do the work and will not need as much training as someone with no similar experience.

Poor Grades

How are/were your grades in school? Not so hot? Employers like job candidates who have a reasonably good academic background and a record of success. Good grades are not only an indicator of your **level of intelligence** and your **capability to learn**, but also thought to be an indicator of your **persistence to succeed** – your motivation to stick to a task, complete it, and do it reasonably well. After all, while you are a student, school **is** your job. If you do/did well in school, employers expect you are likely to do well at work. Really poor grades – mostly D's or F's – are bright red flags! If you lack a record of educational success, be prepared to deal with several red flag questions related to your educational experiences, especially why you had not-so-hot grades.

No Diploma or Degree

Similar to the situation with grades, having a diploma suggests to an employer that you have the capacity to learn and that you stick to a job until it is complete. Having no diploma at an age when most people have been graduated from high school, or failing to pursue a GED, is another red flag. If you attended college or a special school and never completed the degree or certification work, be prepared to explain what may appear to be red flag behaviors – inability to achieve goals, a pattern of failure, behavioral problems, or an unwillingness to stick with challenges. It's one thing to have been expelled from school because of behavioral problems and another thing to have dropped out because of health or financial problems.

> *Your educational background is a good indicator of your capacity to learn and persist.*

lems. As you'll see in Chapter 8, it's important that you address such red flag concerns as positively as possible.

Been Fired

If you have been fired from a past job, hoist a red flag up the flagpole. A potential employer is going to have real concerns about what kind of problem(s) you will bring to his company. Were you fired because you didn't do the job? Because you didn't show up for work or were always late? Because you couldn't get along with your boss? Because you couldn't get along with the other employees or clients? Did you steal from your employer or cheat him? Any or all of these possibilities will come to mind. What was it you did to get fired? Is it something even worse than the things he has in mind? The prospective employer is afraid your former employer's problems will become his if he hires you. It is easier to knock you out of consideration and hire someone without this type of red flag.

Job Hopper

Except in a few high turnover employment fields, such as restaurants, hospitality, and construction, if you have had several jobs in the last year or two, the interviewer is going to wonder why. He may even wonder if you leave the jobs because you keep getting fired from them. But even if the job changes were totally of your own choosing, it doesn't look good to the employer. It raises questions about your real reasons for leaving, and the assumption has to be that you will continue your pattern of behavior and leave this new job – if you were to be hired – after a short period of time as well. This is yet another situation that raises a red flag.

No Focus to the Jobs Held

Let's say you haven't exactly been a job hopper. You have stayed at each of the jobs you have held for a significant period of time. But as the employer looks at your resume or talks with you during the interview about the past jobs you have held, it is apparent there is no focus. You have done a lot of things in several employment situations but the jobs appear scattered – as if you take almost any job offered – perhaps out of desperation. This lack of focus or continuity will raise a red flag with many employers.

Poor References

Most all of us can identify at least a few people who would write a good recommendation for us, but the recommendations that carry the most weight with employers are those references that come from other employers you have worked for. Many former employers are reluctant to get into the details of employee behavior with prospective employers, because of possible legal issues, such as being sued by the former employee. Consequently, they may only verify employment

> *References that carry the most weight come from employers you have worked with.*

dates when asked about the former employer. However, savvy human resources personnel know how to break through this wall of silence and get at red flag behaviors. Indeed, one of the most revealing questions they ask of former employers is this: *"Would you hire this person again?"* Without going into details and exposing themselves to legal liability, a former employer can frankly answer *"yes"* or *"no"* to this question. A *"no"* or *"I would rather not comment"* speaks volumes about potential problems.

If you have no references or if there are no employers you can count on receiving a good recommendation from – assuming you have held jobs in the past – know that this will raise red flags with the employers you interview with for a future job.

Criminal Record

Having been convicted of a felony, which is a question frequently found on employment applications, will definitely raise red flags. Again, the problem is the assumed pattern of behavior. If you committed a crime in the past and it related to the workplace, such as stealing or assault, an employer may assume you will likely commit a similar crime in the future as well as affect the morale of fellow employees who may worry about your criminal behavior. You'll need to acknowledge responsibility for your previous acts and present a convincing case that your behavior has significantly changed since your conviction.

Over-Qualified

Although it is a problem many might think they would be happy to have, being or appearing over-qualified for a position also will raise a red flag with most employers. Far from being thrilled that they can get a better qualified person (better skills) for the same amount of money they have budgeted for the position, in this situation the employer is skeptical. What's your motivation for taking this job as well as for staying on the job for long? He can't help but wonder why you would be willing to accept a position lower than what your skills/experience qualify you for and wonder what it is that you are not telling him. What deep, dark secrets about your past work life are you keeping from him?

He is also concerned that if hired, you will leave for a better and higher paying position as soon as you have the chance – leaving him to go through the hiring and training processes all over again.

Although anything that raises a question in an employer's mind that you don't overcome in the interview (see Chapter 4) may be a knock-out for your likelihood of being hired, the nine knock-out objections discussed above particularly raise red flags.

Test Your Knock-Out Potential

Respond to the following statements to determine how "not-so-hot" your background may be. Circle the numbers to the right of each statement that best represents your degree of agreement or disagreement:

1 = Strongly agree	4 = Disagree
2 = Agree	5 = Strongly disagree
3 = Uncertain	

1. I have no work experience at all.	1 2 3 4 5
2. I have work experience, but it is doing very different work from what I want to do.	1 2 3 4 5
3. My grades in school were not very good.	1 2 3 4 5
4. I have no high school diploma or GED.	1 2 3 4 5
5. I have been fired from one job.	1 2 3 4 5
6. I have been fired from more than one job.	1 2 3 4 5
7. I have held several jobs in the last year.	1 2 3 4 5
8. The jobs I have held have each been very different from each other in terms of the work to be done and skills required.	1 2 3 4 5
9. I don't have a past employer who would give me a good reference.	1 2 3 4 5
10. I have been convicted of a felony.	1 2 3 4 5

TOTAL   _____

If you circled a "1" or "2" for any of these statements, you may raise a red flag in the eyes of most employers. If your total score is between 10 and 35, you will most likely appear to have a not-so-hot background in the eyes of most employers. You'll need to develop interview strategies to overcome your job market weaknesses. Pay special attention to the material in Chapter 4 that discusses strategies for attempting to lower the height of the red flags on the flagpole as well as the sample questions and answers in Chapter 8!

Identify and Deal With Your Red Flags

The first thing you need to do in dealing with red flags is to identify and acknowledge them as potential job knock-outs. Denying them or making excuses will not help you take corrective actions that can make you more employable. Once you've identified your red flags, the next step is to develop strategies for turning red flags into green lights that tell employers that you will be a good hire. You can start this process by asking yourself the following questions:

1. What questions might an employer ask about my background that could raise red flags about my fitness for the job?

2. What five things about my background could knock me out of consideration for a job?

3. What potential red flag behaviors might I need to re-examine and take greater responsibility for in the future?

4. Why would someone want to hire me?

5. What are my best work characteristics?

3

Clues Employers Look for to Determine Successful "Fit"

I N CHAPTER 1 WE DISCUSSED some of the major things employers look for when they interview candidates for a job. Let's review these for a moment:

1. A person with the skills to do the job
2. A person who will show up (and on time) to do the job
3. A person who gets along well with others

4. A person who is able/willing to follow orders/ directions from the boss
5. A person who will listen to instructions/be willing to learn how things are done here
6. A person who is trustworthy
7. A person who will stay with the company for a while

Looking for Hiring Clues

The question then becomes this: How does the employer determine whether or not a job applicant has the skills to do the job (Quality #1) as well as the pattern of behaviors that demonstrate he will do the job and add positive value to the organization (Qualities # 2-7)? The employer will have to rely on two major sources of information to answer this question:

1. What he can determine from the interview
2. Information he can find out from references - especially former employers

So what will the employer be looking for during the interview to try to determine whether you are the right person for the job? The interviewer will look for verbal responses as well as nonverbal cues to try to determine whether you are right for the job. All the while he will be looking for indications that you are not being completely honest. He wants to determine whether you are conning him - giving him the answers you think he wants to hear in order to get the job.

Verbal Exchange

The verbal part of what the employer is looking for is easy enough to understand - the answers you give to questions and the questions you ask about the job and employer. What you say provides information to the employer. This is verbal. He asks about your skills - what training you have had, what experience you have (if you have held previous jobs), and you answer. He may ask what your grades were like in school, why you left a former job, how

> *The interviewer wants to know if you are conning him – giving answers you think he wants to hear.*

you got along with your boss, what your boss was like to work for, what you liked about the job and what you did not like. You might ask him about the organization, position, clients, and performance expectations. These questions and answers form the verbal exchange - a give and take of information.

Nonverbal Cues

The nonverbal part of the interaction is everything else that takes place along with the words that are spoken. It includes your physical appearance and the way you dress, your tone of voice, your facial expression, your eye contact, how you sit in the chair during the interview, your gestures, and other things you may do with your hands - such as clenching them or fidgeting. Most of what is communicated is nonverbal - some estimates place the amount of nonverbal communication at 90% or more. In fact, most estimates suggest only about 7% of the interchange takes place with the words that are spoken - the verbal level.

The first thing the employer is likely to note is your appearance and the way you are dressed. As he reaches out to shake your hand, he probably will be close enough to smell you, and he may also notice the strength of the handshake. As the interview progresses he will listen to the tone of your voice. He will notice your facial expression, your gestures, your overall body language. All these things will make impressions - either positive or negative - on the interviewer. These impressions tell employers something about your professionalism, competence, honesty, and trustworthiness.

Comparing Verbal and Nonverbal Messages

Two other facts about the nonverbal interaction are important to note. People tend to put greater weight on the nonverbal message than on the verbal message. Why? Because it is easier to control the verbal messages we send than the nonverbal ones. Remember getting a gift you really did not want or like - maybe it was for your birthday? The person who gave you the gift was with you when you opened it. What did you say verbally? *"Aunt Helen, I really hate this sweater."* No, we don't think so. You probably said something verbally that indicated your appreciation and that you liked the gift. At least if you wanted to say nice things, it was easy enough to do so. But the nonverbal was a little harder, wasn't it? Your tone of voice may have lacked real enthusiasm and belied the message you were trying to convey. That is what we mean by it being easier to control the verbal message than the nonverbal one.

So if you say with your words that you want the job and that the 6am starting time is no problem, but your voice lacks enthusiasm and suggests that 6am may be earlier than you can manage, the employer will give more weight to what you are communicating nonverbally.

It is also known that people pay more attention to nonverbal cues when they don't have much information about the other person. And that is exactly the situation both you and the employer are in at the start of the interview. So the employer is listening to the verbal messages and watching for the nonverbal cues that may "give you away."

Appearance and Dress

What will make the first impression on the employer? The first thing he will note is your appearance and the way you are dressed. Before you open your mouth to speak, other people are already sizing you up based on how you look. Fair? Probably not. But reality? Definitely! It happens to all of us. Having a not-so-hot background has nothing to do with this fact of life. As he reaches out to shake your hand, the interviewer will be close enough to smell you, and he will notice if there is body odor or a too heavy scent of cologne or after-shave.

Tone of Voice and Eye Contact

As the interview progresses the employer will listen to the tone of your voice. Is there anger in your voice? Complacency? Enthusiasm? Do you exhibit appropriate, yet positive, facial expression or do you look angry or do you have a "stone face," meaning it is nearly expressionless? Are you able to maintain reasonable eye contact with him or do you look away and avoid his eyes? You know there are sayings in our culture that suggest that if a person cannot look us in the eye they are being less than fully truthful. *"He had shifty eyes"* or *"He couldn't look me in the eye"* both suggest the person being spoken about is lying.

Gestures

Gestures that convey involvement, interest, or enthusiasm will be noticed by the interviewer and be considered a plus. But fidgeting with your hands suggests you are nervous - perfectly normal for a job interview - right? However, the employer may interpret it as a sign of deceit. You are exhibiting nervous mannerisms because you are not telling the truth. If your hand(s) is clenched into a fist, which may be another reaction to the stress of the interview, it may be interpreted as a sign of repressed anger and be perceived as revealing a tendency toward aggression.

Facial Expression

If a person's face conveys anger or appears sullen, it will be interpreted as such and be a negative for that individual's job chances.

If a person's face conveys interest and enthusiasm it will be interpreted in a positive way. But what if a person's face is without expression, or what we may refer to as stone-faced? A lack of expression on one's face is normally interpreted in a negative way. Certainly the individual is not viewed as being interested and this comes down as negative.

Body Language

Your body language can convey to the employer interest or lack of interest. As you sit in the interview, the employer may well interpret slouching posture as an indication you are detached from the situation; in other words you are going through the motions, but are not really very interested in the company or the job. A person who is slouching may even appear less smart than he actually is, or one might say the bulb appears to be burning at only 60 watts rather than 100 watts!

Slumped shoulders, which may accompany a slouching posture, suggest the weight of the world is on the job applicant's shoulders - he has given up and looks nearly beaten. Who wants to hire an applicant who already looks beaten? Arms folded across one's chest is often viewed as a sign the individual has closed himself off and is not open to the other person - at least in the situation in which it occurs.

What's Your True Message?

These are some of the major negative signals, often conveyed unknowingly by a job applicant in an interview. Employers are looking for signs of an applicant's true interest and motivation in a job interview, and both the verbal responses and nonverbal behaviors will be viewed by the employer as he tries to determine how much of what the applicant is telling him is true and how much is not. In Chapter 5 we will look at how you can prepare so your verbal responses can be honest but not stupid - in other words, convey your message in the most positive, yet truthful, way possible. In Chapter 6 we will look at ways you can avoid engaging in nonverbal behaviors that convey negative messages about you, and engage in nonverbal behaviors that will send positive, yet honest, messages in a job interview.

Ask Yourself

Consider the situations/questions below to determine your understanding of things the employer will be looking for when interviewing a potential employee:

1. Why does the employer think nonverbal behaviors may tell him more about a potential employee than his verbal answers to questions?

2. What is the first thing the interviewer is likely to notice about me?

3. If a job applicant verbally indicates he is interested in the company, the work they do, and the job opening, but has no expression on his face and no enthusiasm in his voice, what is the employer likely to decide?

4. On a scale of 1 to 10, how would most employers evaluate my nonverbal communication?

5. What nonverbal behaviors do I need to improve?

4

Turn Red Flags Into Green Lights

T HE MOST IMPORTANT KEY to a successful job interview is preparation. Some job seekers think they can't
prepare because they don't know what the questions
will be, while others are just too lazy to spend the time
to prepare. This is the rest of your life we are talking about. Isn't it
worth your time and effort to prepare to put your best self forward in your job interview?

We want you to be yourself, but we also want you to be your
best self. That's what preparation is all about. It is a lot easier to
think about your responses to questions or consider what points

you want to make about your background ahead of time, rather than when you are under the stress you are likely to feel during the job interview. You can anticipate and prepare for most, if not all, of the questions you will be asked during your job interview.

In Chapters 5 and 6, we look at the more general things anyone should do to prepare for a job interview, but in this chapter we will consider the special situation of how someone with a not-so-hot background can best prepare to meet and hopefully overcome potential objections an employer has to hiring a person whose behaviors in the past have led to some poor life choices. Chapter 8 will provide examples of "honest, but not stupid" answers to questions about a variety of not-so-hot backgrounds.

> *You can anticipate and prepare for most questions you will be asked during your job interview.*

Identify Your Personal Red Flags

You know if you have done things in the past that put you in the category of having a difficult background. Nine things that often create objections to hiring a job applicant were listed in Chapter 2. Let's review them:

1. Applicant has little or no experience
2. Applicant had poor grades in school
3. Applicant has no high school diploma
4. Applicant was fired from a previous job
5. Applicant has a pattern of job-hopping
6. Applicant's past jobs show no focus or progression
7. Applicant has poor references
8. Applicant has a criminal record
9. Applicant is over-qualified

While these are some of the most common bases for objections, you may have something in your background that is not listed here. If you think it may be a red flag knock-out factor that will work against you with an employer, put it on your list - even if it isn't listed here.

Start by doing an honest assessment of your past behaviors that might affect your employability. To complete the activity below, next to each number list the major things you have done that you believe will be a red flag to an employer. You may have only one thing on your list or you may have several. Start by just listing the red flag behaviors on the numbered lines. Skip the lines marked A and B until you have listed all the red flag knock-out things you can think of.

1. RED FLAG BEHAVIOR #1: _____

_____

A. Give reason(s) why the behavior listed above happened.

_____

_____

_____

B. Indicate what has changed in the situation/why you will not do it again.

_____

_____

_____

2. RED FLAG BEHAVIOR #2: _____

_____

A. Give reason(s) why the behavior listed above happened.

_____

_____

_____

B. Indicate what has changed in the situation/why you will not do it again.

_____

_____

_____

3. RED FLAG BEHAVIOR #3: _____

_____

A. Give reason(s) why the behavior listed above happened.

_____

_____

_____

B. Indicate what has changed in the situation/why you will
not do it again.

_____

_____

_____

4. RED FLAG BEHAVIOR #4: _____

_____

A. Give reason(s) why the behavior listed above happened.

_____

_____

_____

B. Indicate what has changed in the situation/why you will
not do it again.

_____

_____

_____

5. RED FLAG BEHAVIOR #5: _____

_____

A. Give reason(s) why the behavior listed above happened.

_____

_____

_____

B. Indicate what has changed in the situation/why you will
    not do it again.

_____

_____

_____

Next, go back to each red flag behavior you have listed and
write down the reasons why it happened in the spaces marked A.
Let's say, for example, that one of your red flag behaviors is that
you were fired from a previous job. So you write that on one of the
numbered lines. After you have written down all the red flag behaviors that apply to you, then go back and begin answering part
A for each behavior. Here the question is why? If you were fired
from a job, why were you fired? Was it because you didn't show
up for work or showed up late? Was it because you didn't get
along with your boss or your co-workers? Was it because you
wouldn't follow orders? Did you steal from your employer or lie to
him? Or was it because you were too closely associated with a

senior-level person who left the company? **Are you going to re-peat these behaviors with your next employer?**

Does your employment record indicate you are a job hopper? Why? Why have you had so many jobs over a relatively short period of time? Remember when you are looking at the time you have spent in various jobs that you are looking at this from the employer's point of view - not yours. Three jobs in a year may not seem unreasonable to you, but changing jobs every three or four months will certainly raise questions in the employer's mind. **Are you going to repeat this behavior and leave your next employer after three or four months?**

> *Making excuses or blaming others for your problems is often a sign of not taking respon-sibility for your actions.*

Do you have a criminal record? Why? What did you do? **Are you likely to repeat this behavior?** Have you ever had a problem with drugs or alcohol? Why? **Are you really rehabilitated or are there likely to be problems that will affect your work on your next job?**

It's important that you address each of these red flags as honestly as possible. Making excuses or blaming others for your problems is often a sign of a more serious behavioral problem that most likely affects your relationships with employers, co-workers, clients, family, and friends - not taking responsibility for your actions. Taking responsibility for your not-so-hot background is the first step to making changes in your behavior as well as your career and life.

Questions That Follow Red Flags

You have probably noticed a pattern here. When a red flag is raised, the next question in the employer's mind is why? Why did you engage in that behavior? The question that invariably follows the *"Why"* question in the employer's mind is, *"Are you likely to repeat that behavior - are you going to do it again?"* These follow-up questions, *"Why?"* and *"Will you do it again?,"* may or may not be posed verbally, but they are definitely on the employer's mind. So you will need to respond to these questions - whether or not they are actually asked - if you want to have a chance at getting the job offer.

Prepare to Lower the Red Flag

Remember, the employer is looking for knock-out factors - things that make him decide he doesn't want to take a chance with you. The employer takes a chance with every new employee hired. So you need to consider the employer's concerns about your background, and then truthfully promote yourself by responding to these concerns in an honest, but positive, way.

> *Employers look for knock-out factors - clues about your behavior that tell them it's best not to hire you.*

Why were you fired? If you were fired because you were frequently absent or late for work, you should have put that down. But this raised a follow-up "why" question. Why were you absent or late for work so often? Was it because you were out late the night before? Why were you out late the night before? Were you partying late into the night or were you working a second job and had the night shift? Or were you also a student and you were studying late into the night?

Now that you have responded to as many whys as the situation is likely to raise in the mind of the employer, go on to the third part for each red flag behavior - part B. Why will this not happen again? Now as you look at the possible responses suggested above for the employee being absent or late for work, it may at first look to you like only one - out late partying the night before - is not excusable. Whoa there; you are thinking like the employee - not the employer. Even though out partying probably looks worse than the other reasons to the employer, remember, to the employer, if the work does not get done because the employee is constantly late or absent, it doesn't matter how good the reason for the absence may seem. The bottom line is the same. The work did not get done. The employer you are interviewing with wants to know that this behavior has changed, and needs to be convinced because of the reasons why you say it has changed. Without reasons to support your assertion as to why the behavior has changed, you are likely to be viewed as simply trying to con the employer into hiring you.

So ask yourself what things in your situation have truly changed since you engaged in the problem behavior? What truthful things can you tell the employer to help convince him that you no longer are engaging or will engage in the red flag behavior?

For example, the completed section for one red flag behavior for the hypothetical employee above might look like this:

1. **Red flag behavior #1:** <u>I was fired from job at ABC Motor Repair.</u>

   A. **Give reason(s) why the behavior listed above happened.** <u>I showed up for work late too many days and my boss fired me.</u>

   B. **Indicate what has changed in the situation/why you will not do it again.** <u>I realize it is not a good excuse that I was late for work so often, and that the boss had to have someone he could count on to be at work so the job could get done. At the time this happened I was working a second job and I got off work from the one job at 1:00am, I was supposed to start work at my second job at 6:00am. Taking the commute time for both jobs into consideration,</u>

which totaled about an hour, that left about three and a half hours for sleep each night. After a few weeks, the lack of sleep caught up with me and I am afraid I let my employer down. I can assure you that it will not happen again. I had taken the second job to help pay off my student loans. That debt is now taken care of, and I am able to live within my means. I assure you that if you hire me, you will find me to be a responsible employee whom you can count on. I realize the importance of being on the job each day and on time in order that the work gets done.

Notice what this employee has done as he addresses this red flag behavior:

1. He frankly and truthfully explained the situation.

2. He noted that he understood his employer needed a worker who was on time for work each day.

3. He respected his former employer's decision by not making excuses or negative comments about the employer who fired him.

4. He takes responsibility by explaining why he was late, what corrective actions he took, and notes the situation he was in at the time no longer exists.

5. He again stresses his understanding of the employer's needs - an employee who is on the job each day and on time so that the work gets done.

> *Talking too much about a sensitive issue relating to your behavior or a previous employer can hurt your chances of landing the job.*

This employee, even though he was fired from a previous job, has a good chance of being hired if he has the skills to do the job he has applied for, because he has said the right things to make the prospective employer believe he understands why he was fired, holds no animosity toward the former employer who fired him, and his situation has changed. The thing that created the former problem no longer exists.

Note too that he makes his point in a concise, straightforward, and factual manner. This is not the time to ramble on and on about the situation and blame others. In fact, talking too much about a sensitive issue or situation relating to your behavior or a previous employer can hurt your chances of landing the job.

Get Rid of the Red Flag(s)

Once you have identified your personal red flags, the reason(s) why the behavior took place, and what has changed about your situation so that you can demonstrate it won't happen again, you are ready to formulate the "gist" of the responses or comments you will make to the prospective employer about your red flag situations.

> *Be sure to explain what has changed or what you did to change your situation.*

Planning the "gist" does not mean that you are going to memorize a response or comment; rather, you are deciding the general way in which you will talk about this particular aspect of your life. Ask yourself what you can say to the employer that is honest, yet positive, about how you handled or are handling the situation now. It's important that you explain what has changed or what you did to change your situation. In so doing, you reveal some important elements in your character that are desired by employers - honesty, integrity, forthrightness, responsibility, change, and self-transformation.

Plan the Gist of Your Explanations

Plan the "gist" response or comment you want to make to an employer for each of the red flag situations you identified. Don't try to memorize word for word. If you memorize, chances are you will forget it or it will sound "canned" or both. Neither will be convincing to the employer. Be familiar with the gist of what you want to say and then convey that to the employer in the words that come naturally to you when you are in the interview. You want to convey:

- what changed in your situation
- what you have done to overcome the negative behavior
- what you learned from the experience

In the example we have been following of the applicant who had been fired by his boss at ABC Motors, the situation had changed in that he was now only working one job rather than two. His former situation had him trying to manage on 3½ hours of sleep a night. Now he could get a full night's sleep and get up in time to be at work on time. He had learned how important it is to the employer to have workers on the job each day and on time so that the work gets done.

Keep the following things in mind as you plan your gist response or comments.

Advice: There are many different ways to tell the truth. Keep it honest, but not stupid - tell the truth in the most positive manner possible, but do not confess more than is necessary.

Avoid: Blurting out all your weaknesses or negatives; the job interview is not the time nor place for "true confessions." Keep your comments related to the work situation. Your situation at home, as long as it does not affect the work you are doing, is none of the employer's business.

Advice: Keep your comments concise, focused, and to the point.

Avoid: Talking too much, rambling on and on out of nervousness. A little silence is all right.

We have discussed planning the gist of your responses to questions or comments you wish to make. If you believe the employer is hesitant about something in your background, but he isn't asking you about it, you can bring it up yourself. If you have a positive explanation for a red flag behavior, why would you leave that hesitancy in the employer's mind? It will likely grow as a negative factor as the employer weighs your candidacy against other applicants for the job. You not only can, but should, bring it up if you believe you have a positive explanation that will help your chances:

"You are aware that I was fired from my job at ABC Motors. I would like to explain the situation and what I have done to make sure this never happens again."

If you are going to bring up a red flag behavior, don't wait until the end of the interview to do so, and you certainly don't want to begin with it either. The beginning and the end of the interview are most likely to be remembered with greater clarity by the employer. So try to end on the most positive note possible.

5

Prepare to Meet the Employer's Needs:
The Verbal Exchange

THE KEY WORDS IN THIS chapter's title are "prepare" and "employer's needs." Preparation is not only possible, it is necessary to put your best self forward in the interview. This is true for any job applicant, but especially so for an applicant with red flags in his background. Since the job interview is the crucial step to getting a job offer, it's extremely important that you prepare well for the interview. What you say and do during the interview may well overcome any deficiencies in your background. Above all, the employer needs to feel confident that he is making the right hiring decision.

Meeting the employer's needs means that you should try to determine what the company's needs are rather than viewing the interview only from your own perspective of needs and wants. We looked at many of the generic needs employers have today in the first chapter when we discussed what employers want in today's market. You may wish to return to Chapter 1 to review the general needs most employers have in common.

Research the Company and the Job

Find out as much about the company as you can. Start by checking the Internet for information on the company. Be sure to visit the company's website. Many company websites provide a wealth of information on operations, including profiles of key personnel and helpful hints on applying for a job. If you don't have personal access to the Internet, find a friend who does or use the Internet connections at your local library.

> *Many company websites provide a wealth of information on operations.*

Do you know people who work at the company or have worked there in the past? Talk to them about what the company does, what it is like to work there, what kind of jobs they offer. Ask as many specific questions as come to mind. For example, when asking what it is like to work there, what do you really want to know? What are the normal working hours? What is the opportunity for overtime? Or, how much overtime is mandated? What is the likelihood you will asked to take any tests during the interview stage? How many paid holidays are there? Sick leave? Vacation days? What other benefits does the company offer? Ask questions about working for the company as well. What is/was the person's boss like? Are employees' concerns listened to and taken into account? Has the company been facing any problems lately–with sales, product line, competition from foreign firms? Your data-gathering questions generally cover four categories:

questions about what you might expect at a job interview; questions about benefits; questions about what it is like to work there; and questions about problems the company may face.

If you know what the job opening is, ask questions about the particular job you will be applying for. This is the time you can ask questions concerning your own self-interests. Once you are in the job interview, questions concerning job benefits should not be asked at least until the end of the interview, and many job search authorities would advise you not to ask these self-interest centered benefit questions until

> *This is the time you can ask questions concerning your own self-interests.*

you have been offered the job. During the job interview you should focus on the employer's needs and how you can fill that need.

In addition to asking questions of people you know who work or have worked for the company, there are other sources of information. There are often printed materials about companies - especially large or publicly held companies - which you can find in your local library. Make friends with the librarian, who can be helpful in assisting you to locate materials that are available. Perhaps easiest of all is to go online. There are few companies these days, even very small ones, that do not have a website. Look over the website carefully and you are likely to find information that will help you during your interview. Look for information about officers or managers; information about the product lines or services they provide; and information about the financial health of the organization.

Match Your Goals/Strengths to the Employer's Needs

The more you know about the job opening and how the job fits into the company's overall product line or service offerings, the better you can determine your fit - how your skills and experience will mesh with the employer's needs. Prepare to be able to talk about this "fit" during the interview. Practice the "gist" of what you might say in a minute or two to convince the employer of how your skills/experience meet the company's needs. Don't try to memorize it - just be familiar with the main points you want to make.

Prepare to Complete an Application or Test

For many jobs, if you have a resume you will not be expected to fill out a job application. Other employers will require you to complete an application whether or not you have a resume. Not only does the completed application provide necessary information to

> *The application you complete tells the employer a lot more about you than might be apparent at first glance.*

the employer, but how you fill it out speaks volumes as well. Do you understand the questions? Do you fill out the application completely or do you leave some spaces blank? How do you respond to sensitive questions that could be potential job knock-outs, such as *"Have you ever been convicted of a felony? If yes, explain."* Do you complete the application reasonably neatly? What about spelling and grammar? In other words, the application you complete in the employer's office tells the employer a lot more about you than might be apparent at first glance.

Before you leave home for the interview, anticipate the questions you may be asked to complete on an application form: education completed and relevant dates; former jobs held including the name of the company and its address and phone number, relevant dates, and the name of your immediate supervisor; if you are a veteran, dates served in the military, date of discharge, type of discharge, and other relevant information; names and contact information for references you may be asked to provide. Take your social security card, since some employers may want to see it. These things constitute the minimum information you should take with you to the job interview. You may think of other things that are pertinent to your situation, such as any on-the-job training or courses you completed while employed elsewhere.

Consider carefully the people you will use as references. The strongest references from the employer's viewpoint will come from individuals in the business community - ideally individuals who have some familiarity with the work you do even though you may not have worked for them or have done so in a non-traditional way. For example, if you mowed lawns for several prominent business people when you were younger and impressed them with your energy and drive or perhaps your attention to detail, those persons would be good references even though you did not work for them in their company. If you are recently out of school and have little or no work experience, a teacher might make a good reference.

> *Consider carefully the people you will use as references. Ask their permission to use them as references.*

Once you have determined who your strongest references will be, ask their permission to use them as a reference. This is considered the proper way to deal with personal references, and it will further impress upon the individual whose support you want that you are a conscientious person who does things properly. This contact with the potential reference serves other purposes as well. It gives the individual a chance to decline your request if he feels he cannot give you a good recommendation. It also provides an opportunity for you to review your strengths you hope your reference will mention on your behalf. If this person is aware of red flags you have in your past, it gives you the opportunity to remind your potential reference how you have changed your situation and overcame, or are working on overcoming, your past problems.

Take all the contact information on your references - their names correctly spelled; their title, if applicable; addresses; and their phone numbers - with you to the job interview so you can accurately fill out an application if you are asked to complete one. Remember to also take information about your education, past jobs, military service, and any specialized training you may have received with you to the interview in order to complete questions about these areas accurately on an application.

Prepare for Questions

You know you will be asked questions during the job interview. You may be asked personal questions, questions about your education, about your experience, about your failures, about your accomplishments, about what motivates you, and about your future goals or plans. Again, it is important that you prepare for the questions you are most likely to face. Yes, it will take time to prepare. But if it isn't worth your effort to prepare to do well in the interview, why waste your time going to the interview at all?

You can anticipate most of the questions you are likely to be asked. Sit down and make a list of those you can expect, and don't forget to include questions about any red flags in your past, as you detailed in Chapter 4. Use the following general list to divide the questions into categories. We suggest a few questions areas in each category below. But you should add additional ones that apply to your personal experience. Chapter 9 includes an expanded version of this list in bulleted format.

Questions I am Likely to be Asked by Category

- Questions about my personal life
- Questions about my education
- Questions about my work experience

- Questions about my accomplishments and work style
- Questions about what motivates me
- Questions about my future goals/plans

Questions About Your Personal Life

Because many personal questions are illegal to ask in an employment interview, you may be asked questions that are indirect. For example, rather than to ask your age, which is illegal, the interviewer may ask when you graduated, which is legal, and from which he can estimate your age. It is illegal to ask, whether on the application form or in the interview, whether you ever committed a crime, but it is legal to ask if you have ever been convicted of a felony. If you

> *Never try to memorize an answer.*

have a period of time during which you were neither in school nor employed, this will raise questions in the mind of the employer and he will no doubt ask what you were doing during that time period.

Whatever the question the employer is likely to ask, whether it is about a red flag in your background or something else, you will do far better answering the question if you have anticipated the question and thought through the "gist" of your response. Again, do not try to memorize an answer. Instead, consider your strategy in answering the question. What can you say that is honest, yet puts you in the most positive light? It is far easier, less stressful, and your answer will no doubt say more positive things about you if you can think through your strategy in the more relaxed atmosphere of your home than if you encounter the question for the first time during the job interview.

Questions About Your Education

Be prepared for questions about your education. If your grades were not so hot, be prepared to talk about that. Did you just goof off or were you working several hours a week at a part-time job? You may be asked what classes you liked the most or the least when you were in school. If you were not graduated from high school (do not have a high school diploma) be prepared to explain why you dropped out without completing high school and whether you are pursuing (or plan to pursue) a GED (General Equivalent Diploma). For employers, many questions relating to education are good indicators of a candidate's intelligence, goals, decision-making style, and tenacity.

Questions About Your Experience

Do you have any work experience? Any experience that relates to the job for which your are applying? Obviously, related experience is most helpful, and if you have experience that relates to the job you are seeking, you should mention that and be sure to go further and explain the similarities to the interviewer.

Even if your past job(s) do not directly relate, you still have positive connections you can make. If, for example, you had a good record of attendance, were always on the job and on time at your previous job, if you have a good recommendation from your former employer(s), this evidence of positive behaviors on a former job - whether part-time, full-time, or volunteer work – helps establish that you are likely to be a good worker for another employer.

Questions About Your Accomplishments and Work Style

What are your greatest strengths? What do you do well and enjoy doing? What is your greatest weakness? What kind of jobs do you not enjoy doing? What things about you, yourself, would you like to improve? Do you lose your temper easily? Do your prefer working with others as a team or alone?

Don't be shy talking about your strengths. Stress the things you have accomplished. Think about the things you do well and enjoy doing. Can you relate these strengths to aspects of the job you are applying for? If asked about your weaknesses, try to mention something the interviewer already knows, something that does not relate to the job, or something you have changed for the better. If you have red flag behaviors in your background, but have turned things around and made significant improvements, this may be an excellent opportunity to stress the positive changes you have made in your life and in your behavior.

Questions About Your Goals and Motivation

Employers look for candidates who are highly motivated to do the job, establish a record of accomplishments, and advance their careers. They want self-motivated individuals who have employer-centered goals rather than self-centered goals. Asking questions about your motivations gives them clues as to what will motivate you to succeed in their company. Do they need to constantly supervise you in order to get work done or are you a self-starter who is motivated to do a good job with minimum

> *Employers want self-motivated individuals who have employer-centered goals rather than self-centered goals.*

supervision and on-the-job incentives? You may be asked, for example, about what you learned from your previous job(s). If your application or resume shows you have left a previous job(s), you are likely to be asked why. Be prepared to talk about why you want to work for this company as well as why you want this job. You may even be asked, *"Why should I hire you?"*

Questions About Your Future Goals/Plans

Do you have plans for future education? Plans to change the kind of work you do? How long do you plan to stay in this job - if we hire you? What do you see yourself doing 5 or 10 years from now?

Practice for the Interview

Be honest, but not stupid. There are many ways to tell the truth. Think about the questions suggested here as well as any others you might be asked based on the information provided on your resume or that you expect to be asked based on the information you will fill out on your application. Consider how you would best respond to each of these questions. Do not memorize responses. Just think about the strategy you would use, the "gist" of the response you would make to be as honest as possible, yet as positive as possible. We

> *Be honest, but not stupid. There are many ways to tell the truth. Make sure your truth puts the best light on you.*

hear political pundits talk about "putting a positive spin" on a situation. How can you put a positive spin on your responses without being dishonest? We frequently tell job seekers to "be honest, but not stupid." In other words, don't lie - it will only come back to haunt you. But neither should you decide this is the time to "come clean" and confess about everything negative you have ever done in your life. There are many ways to tell the truth. Make sure your truth puts the best light on you.

Respond to questions as fully and in as positive a manner as you truthfully can, then know when to stop talking and let the interviewer ask a follow-up question or move on.

Ask Yourself

1. What sources of information are likely to be available to me about a company where I may have an interview?

2. I am interested in the benefits (pay, vacation/sick leave, health insurance, etc.) that come with the job. Why shouldn't I ask about benefits early in the job interview?

3. Why is it important that I ask my potential references for their permission to use them as a reference?

4. Whose opinion of me (my family members, my teachers, my former employers, or a businessperson I formerly worked for - such as yard work as a teenager) will likely carry the most weight for a reference for a job?

5. Why is it important for me to anticipate questions I may be asked during the job interview, and consider the strategy I would use and the gist of my response?

6

Nonverbal Behaviors That Meet Needs and Exceed Expectations

W
HAT YOU SAY VERBALLY during the interview relays a lot of information about you, the job applicant, to the interviewer. Whether you are aware of it or not, you are also communicating information nonverbally. In Chapter 3, we discussed many kinds of nonverbal behavior and the reasons why nonverbal is perceived as being more honest than the messages communicated verbally. Because it is more difficult to control our nonverbal behavior, it is more difficult for us to intentionally manipulate and convey false messages. Thus, nonverbal behavior is thought to be more honest or more

reflective of the real feelings of the communicator - in this case the job applicant.

So let's look at how you can prepare to present your best self to the employer in the job interview nonverbally.

Manage Your Physical Appearance and Dress - Men

The first thing the interviewer will notice is your physical appearance and the way you dress. Before you open your mouth to speak, the employer is already making judgments about you. These judgments concern your competence, whether you are trustworthy, whether you would be a good "fit" in the organization. How can he determine these things just by looking at you? He can't. But he makes judgments and comes to conclusions about you just the same. We all do it. You have done it too - about your teachers in school, potential employers, and people you meet on the street. Whether it is fair or not, it is reality. Know that the interviewer is sizing you up as soon as he sees you. Make this fact of life work for you by planning and managing your appearance and dress to work to your advantage. Make your appearance convey positive things about you.

> *The first thing the interviewer notices is your appearance and dress.*

Make certain you are clean and neatly groomed from head to toe. You are freshly showered, including clean and combed hair. You smell good, but your scent is not overpowering. You have applied deodorant (not optional) and perhaps a light cologne (optional). If you use a scent, do not apply it with a heavy hand. A strong scent can be a real turn-off and work against you. If hired, you will be working with these people daily. The negatives of body odor or an overpowering cologne could be enough to lose you the job opportunity. Your fingernails are trimmed and clean. Your teeth are freshly brushed and you have used mouthwash. You should be freshly shaven.

Your clothing is clean, neat, and relatively conservative. This is not the time to emulate the dress of your favorite rock star. The most dressed down attire for a man is a freshly laundered and pressed (or a fabric that looks pressed) shirt and clean pair of slacks. Wear socks, even if it isn't "cool," and polished shoes. This clean and neat but dressed down attire would be appropriate if you are applying for a job stocking shelves, working in an auto-repair facility, or a similar type of job.

If you are applying for a job other than in a blue collar field, dress the outfit up a bit by adding a sport jacket and necktie. Of course, for a white collar job, a suit and tie would be most appropriate. You can always dress up to the next higher level than the job you are applying for as long as you feel comfortable. This would be an example of exceeding the employer's expectations.

Manage Your Physical Appearance and Dress - Women

The first thing the interviewer will notice is your physical appearance and the way you dress. Before you open your mouth to speak, the employer is already making judgments about you. These judgments concern your competence, whether you are trustworthy, whether you would be a good "fit" in the organization. How can he determine these things just by looking at you? He can't. But he makes judgments and comes to conclusions about you just the same. We all do it. You have done it too - about your teachers in school, potential employers, and people you meet on the street. Whether it is fair or not, it is reality. Know that the interviewer is sizing you up as soon as he sees you. Make this fact of life work for you by planning and managing your appearance and dress to work to your advantage. Make your appearance convey positive things about you.

Make certain you are clean and neat from head to toe. You are freshly showered and your hair is clean and nicely styled. You smell good. You have applied deodorant (not optional) and if you wish to use a light cologne (optional) you have applied it sparingly. Body odor or a too strong scent can be a real turn-off and work against you. Your fingernails are trimmed and clean. If you use polish, a natural shade is best. A light pink might be acceptable, but, please, no "funky" colors such as purple or green. Your teeth are freshly brushed and you have used a mouthwash.

Your clothing is clean, neat, and relatively conservative. The most dressed down attire for a woman is a freshly laundered and pressed blouse and a clean pair of slacks. Wear polished shoes, flats or a low heel, that match or are darker than the color of the slacks. This is not the time to wear that new pair of clunky clogs or stiletto heels. Shoes that are lighter in color than your slacks will call attention to your feet; you want the interviewer to concentrate on your face. Nylons in a skin tone will best complement your look. This clean and neat but informal attire would be appropriate if you are applying for a job stocking shelves or similar position. If you are applying for most other jobs, or any job where you would have face-to-face contact with customers, dress up a notch. Wear slacks or a skirt and a matching blazer-type jacket or wear a "base" consisting of a top that matches your slacks or skirt and add a contrasting blazer or one that is a plaid with one of the colors in the plaid matching your "base" slack and top color. Low heeled shoes that match or are as dark or darker than your slacks or skirt will look best. If applying for a professional position, your best bet is a skirted suit.

Make Your Body Language Say Positive Things About You

When you first meet the interviewer, your handshake should be firm and strong, but not so strong that you crush the employer's fingers in your grip. Avoid giving a limp handshake. The interviewer will probably indicate with a gesture where you are to sit.

> ## Sit erect and with a very slight forward lean.

Once seated, don't slouch but rather sit erect and even with a very slight forward lean to the upper part of your body. To slouch in your chair conveys a detachment from the situation that suggests this interview isn't really very important to you, you are not interested in what is going on, or even that you are not too bright! To sit erect indicates you are alert, and the slight forward lean into the conversation conveys interest in the proceedings.

No slumped shoulders either. Slumped shoulders suggest that the weight of the world is on your shoulders and you are nearly beaten down. Who wants to hire a beaten down person? No squirming uncomfortably in the chair either. That is distracting to the interviewer, and may even suggest you have something to hide. Try not to fidget with your hands and avoid gestures with closed fists. Fidgeting behavior suggests you are nervous - who wouldn't be in a job interview - and have something to hide. Closed fists may convey aggressiveness.

So what positive signals can you convey through your body language?

DO:

- Sit fairly erect in the chair. This suggests you are alert, interested, and involved.

- Sit with a very slight forward lean to the upper part of your body. This conveys your interest in the conversation and the interviewer.

- Keep your hands open and relaxed so you can gesture when appropriate.

- Avoid clenching your hands together as you are less likely to use them to gesture.
- Avoid clenched fists, which may suggest aggressive behavior.

DON'T:

- Fidget with your hands.

- Squirm (reposition yourself frequently) in the chair.

Gesture frequently if it is natural. Gestures help convey your interest and enthusiasm and help keep the interviewer's attention focused on your message as well.

Eye Contact and Facial Expression

Make frequent, although not constant, eye contact with the interviewer. The applicant who won't look the employer in the eye may be considered uninterested or even dishonest and hiding something. When we say, "He couldn't look me in the eye," we suggest the person had something to hide. "Shifty eyes" is another term used to suggest a person may be less than honest. Look at the employer most

> *Your facial expression should indicate your interest and enthusiasm.*

of the time, looking away occasionally so neither of you feel uncomfortable.

By your facial expression you can indicate your interest and enthusiasm. A positive facial expression does not have to include a smile, but often will. A pleasant look on your face indicating interest is fine. Break into a smile occasionally when it seems appropriate. A smile adds life to most faces, and that life will be perceived as enthusiasm by the interviewer.

Avoid a face that appears angry (a scowl) or a stone face (no expression at all). Obviously, a face that appears angry will not convey positives to the employer, and a face devoid of expression will be interpreted negatively. You will be perceived as lacking interest in the job, the company, and the interviewer.

Vocal Expression

The final way you communicate nonverbally is by your tone of voice. Does your voice have vocal variety that conveys your interest and enthusiasm? Or does a lack of vocal variety (perhaps approaching a monotone) convey a lack of interest or enthusiasm?

Your Total Nonverbal Message

A combination of all the elements of nonverbal messages, taken together, can help or hinder you in the job interview. The way you manage your appearance and dress for the interview communicates to the employer whether you cared enough about the interview to clean up and dress appropriately. A slovenly appearance or inappropriate attire suggests that you either don't know any better, or don't care.

> *You should communicate similar verbal and nonverbal messages. If not, you will confuse the employer.*

Your body language - eye contact, facial expression, and your vocal expressiveness - further conveys your interest or lack of interest throughout the interview. If all the aspects of your nonverbal behavior are congruent - that is, they communicate the same message and that message is the same as your verbal message - then you will communicate a strong message to the interviewer that should be believable. If some of the aspects of your message are at odds with other aspects (for example, you say [verbally] you are interested in the job, but your nonverbal messages suggest otherwise and contradict the verbal), the employer is likely to be confused. You say one thing, but act another. In this case the employer is likely to be uncomfortable with you for the job, and you are likely to lose out on the chance at being hired.

So get your act together and communicate similar messages through your nonverbal behavior as you do with the words you say. Practice responding to expected questions in front of a mirror. What do you see? Is it an interested, enthusiastic job applicant?

For more information on nonverbal behaviors and details on dress and appearance for job interviews, see our two companion books: *Interview for Success* and *Savvy Interviewing: The Nonverbal Advantage* (Impact Publications).

Ask Yourself

1. Why is the job applicant's appearance important for the job interview?

2. Why do people believe nonverbal messages are more truthful than verbal messages?

3. Name at least three ways you can nonverbally communicate to an interviewer that you are interested in the job you are applying for?

7

At the Interview:
Wow the Interviewer

G ETTING TO AND THROUGH the job interview successfully requires several actions on your part. As we stressed in the first six chapters, it's important that you put your best self in the interviewee's chair, overcome red flags in your background, and prepare to win at the job interview. It's also important to pay particular attention to the details of the interview process. When, for example, should you arrive at the interview site? How should you greet the interviewer? What should you be listening for during the interview?

Good Preparation Wins

Preparation takes time, but if winning the job is important to you, it will be time well spent. Look at it this way. Let's say you are applying for a job that pays $10.00 an hour. If you work a 40-hour week for a year, that job will pay you over $20,000 during your first year. Or perhaps you are applying for a $30,000 or $50,000 a year job. Is it worth that much to you to spend time to prepare to do well in your job interview?

Preparation will give you a huge advantage over people who don't prepare.

If you decide to go to the interview and "wing it" - you don't take time to prepare because you are busy, lazy, or think you are so glib you can just talk a lot and fool the interviewer - think again. Chances are the employer has met job candidates like you before, and he will neither be impressed nor fooled.

So do your homework. Put in the necessary time to go through the preparation for the job interview discussed in the previous chapters. It is no guarantee you will be offered every job you apply for, but preparation will give you a huge advantage over people with backgrounds similar to yours who do not take the time to prepare!

Last Minute Advice

Get a good night's sleep the night before your interview. You will feel better, look better, and be able to think more clearly to answer and ask questions of the interviewer if you are well rested.

Arrive at the interview site a bit earlier than the time set for the interview. Do a practice run a day or two before the interview if you are unsure of the location or how long it will take you to get there. Check ahead to find out what parking is available and whether you will have any time-consuming procedures upon arrival such as getting through a security check. Leave yourself plenty of time for problems in either of these areas. If you arrive early you will have time to gather your thoughts rather than worrying about whether you will be late. An early arrival will give you time to visit the restroom - you may need it if you feel nervous, and you can check your appearance in the mirror as well.

> *Never be late for a job interview. Doing so leaves a very bad initial impression from which you may never recover!*

Employers indicate the impression made by an applicant during the first 4-5 minutes of the job interview is seldom changed during the remainder of the interview, even if the interview lasts an half hour or more. You will not make a very good impression on the interviewer during the first 4-5 minutes if you are not even there! If the interview is not important enough to you that you can be prompt, the employer will have serious questions about the likelihood that you will have a good record of being on time if you get the job.

Go alone to the job interview - no friends and no children should accompany you! Both send the wrong message to the employer. Taking a friend to the interview suggests that you may be too dependent on the other person to be a dependable employee in your own right and also unable to work independently. Taking a child with you suggests that child care may be a problem that would interfere with your being on the job each day and on time. If you are dependent on a friend to drive you to the interview, have your friend drop you outside and meet you later rather than accompany you inside to the interview. Make sure, though, that you will be able to get to work each day if you are offered and accept the job.

Entering the Office and Waiting for the Interviewer

When you enter the office where the interview is to take place, introduce yourself to the receptionist. If you know the name of the person with whom you will be meeting, indicate this to the receptionist as well. If not, indicate that you have an appointment and the position you are applying for or the department is in. It is to your advantage to know the name of the person who will interview you. If possible, find out the person's name ahead of time, and be sure to write it down - it is okay to ask how to spell it. This way you can be familiar with the name to tell to the receptionist and you can use the person's name - the last name with the appropriate Mr., Mrs., Ms., Dr., etc. before it - during the interview as well.

> *While waiting in the reception area, read materials that relate to the company or job.*

Before you take a seat in the reception area to wait for your interview, try to get rid of any outdoor gear you may have with you: an outdoor-type coat, boots, or umbrella. Leave these things in the reception area if possible. Carrying them into the interview with you is awkward; it is hard to shake hands when you meet the interviewer with an umbrella in your hand. Wearing a coat into the interview makes you appear uncomfortable and as if you are ready to leave. It marks you as an outsider, since the people who belong there, the employees, are not dressed in outdoor attire.

While waiting in the reception area, review materials you brought with you if you wish, or read materials about the company if available. Reading about the company may provide information that will aid you during the interview - either help you answer questions or give you ideas for thoughtful questions you might wish to ask. If there are no company materials available, then pick up a business or news magazine while you wait. What you are seen reading also makes a statement about you, so read something worthwhile.

As the Interview Begins

When you meet the interviewer, stand up if you have been seated waiting in the reception area, smile, extend your hand, and call him or her by name if you know the person's name. Follow the interviewer from the reception area to an office, conference room, or work area where the interview will take place. Usually the interviewer will

> *Sit with a very slight forward lean toward the interviewer.*

motion toward the chair where you should seat yourself. Wait for a moment for the interviewer to do this rather than just taking a seat.

Remember the nonverbal behaviors (Chapter 6) you know are important and sit fairly erect in the chair - not like a soldier at attention, but certainly not slouching. Sit with a very slight forward lean toward the interviewer if you feel comfortable doing this. You should especially lean forward if you are particularly interested in what is being discussed or are making a point with enthusiasm. Maintain moderate eye contact with the interviewer. Try not to fidget or clench your hands together, but keep your hands relaxed and open - all the better to gesture with when you are making a point.

During the Interview

Let the interviewer begin. Listen carefully to what he says so you can learn as much as possible about the job and so you will be ready to respond to questions he may ask you. If you have prepared, you should be ready for most of the questions you are likely to be asked. If you are asked a question you were not expecting, don't panic. Ask him to repeat the question, or probe for what the interviewer wants if you are unsure.

For example, if the interviewer asks you to tell him about your background, you could probe by asking whether he would like you to talk about your education or your experience. Or you could pick whichever part of your background you believe is stronger, let's say you pick your experience, talk about that briefly as it relates to the job, and

> *Sell yourself as you answer questions posed by the interviewer.*

then ask whether that was what he was looking for or whether he would also like to know about some other aspect - such as your education. The important thing is that you don't panic. Stay calm. Think what strength relates to the question asked and go with that. If he wants other information, he can ask a follow-up question.

View the interview as a two-way street. Yes, the interviewer is trying to learn about you and your potential "fit" for the job. But you need to learn as much as you can about the job - both so you can ask intelligent questions during the interview and so later, if you are offered the job, you can make your own decision about whether the job is a good "fit" for you.

Take, and perhaps even make, opportunities to sell yourself. Yes, you sell yourself as you answer questions posed by the interviewer. But if you have a real strength that relates to the job, and it doesn't seem as if the interviewer is going to ask a question that gives you the chance to sell this point, make the opportunity. Say to the interviewer, *"Let me tell you about ..."* or *"That situation reminds me of what I did at ..."* or *"When I worked at ..."* or whatever seems like a transition that gives you a chance to sell your skills, your experience, or your talent.

Listen for Underlying Messages and Questions

Of course you know you should listen to what the interviewer says and the questions you are asked. But listen at a second underlying level as well. What does the interviewer really want to know? Is the interviewer probing to try to get at the answers to questions that he is hesitant to ask or cannot ask because the questions would get into areas that are illegal to ask about?

But, you may say, if there is an area that it is illegal for the employer to ask me about, why should I volunteer information? I do not have to do that. The law is there to protect me. You are right; there are certain kinds of information you do not have to reveal. But the employer has rights too, and one of those rights is to decide not to hire you. It may often be to your advantage to choose to deal with areas of your background that you know the employer may not legally ask you about, but may know or find out about - especially if you can put a positive spin on it!

For example, an employer has the right to be interested in whether you have dependable child care so that you will be at work and on time on a regular basis. He might indirectly get to that question by asking if you anticipate any difficulties in coming to work at 8am and leaving no earlier than 5pm each day. Or he might ask if you foresee any problems in working overtime or coming in on weekends. Since you may suspect he is probing about your family situation, you might want to volunteer this information in a positive manner that also gives you information on how the employer treats employees who have a family life:

> *"I do have family obligations. But I can be flexible since I have a very supportive family. They know my work is important, and my employer usually knows how important my family is to me. I don't foresee a problem. What has been your experience in working with employees who have family obligations? Would you say this is a family-friendly company?"*

So if you have red flag areas in your background, and the employer is likely to find out about them or will at least have indications from your resume, your interview, or your references that there may be problem areas, you are usually better off to address the potential concerns in as honest, yet positive, a manner as you can.

Dealing With Questions About a Difficult Background

Prior to the interview you have anticipated areas of questioning that may involve things in your past that probably will not be plus factors in an employer's hiring decision. If you did not complete high school, are likely to receive negative comments about your work or work habits from a former employer, have a record of job hopping, have been fired from a job, have a criminal record or a record that includes alcohol or drug abuse, you must be prepared to address questions or even raise the issue yourself to put the red flag to rest and have a chance at being hired.

We will deal with specific questions and strategies for handling questions on difficult backgrounds in Chapter 8. For now, let's look at some general guidelines for dealing with questions about red flag behaviors.

- Give the information asked for - no more. This is not the time to confess all your past negative behaviors. Talking too much draws excessive attention to your negatives.

- Maintain good eye contact throughout. Remember, you do not want to seem dishonest by not looking the interviewer in the eye.

- Talk briefly about what you have learned from the mistake you made in the past. Acknowledge and take responsibility for your actions.

- Talk about what you have done to change this aspect of your life. What have you done to modify the red flag situation and behavior as well as what positive behavior(s) have you put in place? Your future is different than your past.

- Make your comments positive and concise. Do not ramble on and on.

- If you are the one bringing up the subject of a red flag behavior, avoid introducing the subject early in the interview. You want to have the chance to impress the interviewer with your positive attributes and make a favorable first favorable impression. Also, avoid introducing the subject of a red flag behavior at the very end of the interview unless you have overcome the problem in a truly significant way. You want the final thing the interviewer remembers about you to be positive.

Accentuate the Positive

> *Support your positive statements with examples – they will be remembered.*

You can stress your positives in part by what you say about yourself. Use positive words such as "*I can . . . , I am interested in . . . , I have done that . . . , I was successful doing that . . . ,*" Avoid negative or tentative words such as "*I can't . . . , I wouldn't . . . , or I might . . .*"

Make your statements positive and sell your strengths and your good "fit" for the job. Use specific examples when you can:

> *"At my job at ABC Co. I suggested a way to streamline stocking the shelves, and the company achieved 20% greater efficiency in this area. I was even named 'Employee of the Year'. I think my success at ABC Co. makes me a great fit for your opening in the stockroom here at XYZ Co.! I am really excited about the opportunity."*

Support your positive statements with examples, if possible. The facts you share make your statements more credible, better understood, more interesting, and better remembered. You want to be remembered and want your accomplishments to be remembered after the interview is over.

Make sure your tone of voice and facial expression express the same interest and enthusiasm as your verbal message.

Ask Yourself

1. Why are the first 4-5 minutes of the job interview so important?

2. What materials should you read while waiting in the reception area to meet the interviewer?

3. Why is it important to share examples of my past positive accomplishments with the interviewer?

4. Why might I want to mention a red flag behavior in my past if the employer doesn't bring it up?

8

Avoid 35 Common Interview Errors

C ONGRATULATIONS! YOU'VE BEEN invited to a job interview. Your job search efforts have finally paid off. Now go into that job interview, sell yourself, and get the job offer. However, that's easier said than done. The very thought of going to a job interview touches on a full range of emotions - joy at getting the interview and sweaty palms thinking about what to wear, say, and do during the interview. You will be facing a critical audience who will ask you many probing questions to determine whether or not to offer you the job. There are many things you might say or do that could knock you out of further consideration.

It's a Very Stressful Time

The job interview is one of the most stressful situations you may encounter. As we noted in previous chapters, the interview is more than just talk centering on a series of questions and answers. It's also about making a good impression, from what you wear and how you smell to the way in which you greet potential employers, maintain eye contact during the interview, and close and follow up the interview. Do you

Interview errors tend to be unforgiving.

communicate confidence and trustworthiness in your demeanor, or are you that interviewee who has a limp handshake and shifty eyes? How do you dress, what do you say, and how do you handle yourself throughout various phases of the interview process? You're on stage and your audience is judging you with a very critical eye.

Mistakes You Shouldn't Make

Unlike many other job search mistakes, interview errors tend to be unforgiving. This is the time when first impressions count the most.

Employers have both positive and negative goals in mind. On the positive side, they want to hire someone who can do the job and add value or benefits to their organization. On the negative side, they are always looking for clues that tell them why they should not hire you. It's not until you start performing on the job that the employer gets to see the "real you" and discover your patterns of behavior. In the meantime, the employer needs to be on his or her guard looking for evidence that you may be the wrong person for the job. Make a mistake during the job interview and you may be instantly eliminated from further consideration. Therefore, you must be on your very best behavior and avoid the many common mistakes interviewees make.

The following mistakes are frequently cited by employers who have interviewed hundreds of applicants:

1. **Arrives late to the interview.** First impressions really do count and they are remembered for a long time. Arrive late and you've made one of the worst impressions possible! Indeed, regardless of what you say or do during the interview, you may never recover from this initial mistake. Employers wonder, *"Will you also come to work late?"*

2. **Makes a bad impression in the waiting area.** Treats receptionists and secretaries as inferiors - individuals who may have important input into the hiring process when later asked by the employer *"What was your impression of this candidate?"* Caught reading frivolous materials - *People Magazine* - in the waiting area when company reports and related literature were readily available.

3. **Offers stupid excuses for behavior.** Excuses are usually red flags indicating that a person is unwilling to take responsibility and do the work. Here's a killer excuse for arriving late for a job interview: *"I got lost because your directions weren't very clear."* Goodbye! Here are some other classic excuses heard during job interviews:

   - *I forgot.*
   - *It wasn't my fault.*
   - *It was a bad company.*
   - *My boss was a real jerk.*
   - *The school wasn't very good.*
   - *I can't remember why I did that.*
   - *No one there appreciated my work.*
   - *I didn't have time to visit your website.*
   - *I'm not a job hopper - I'm just getting lots of good experience and advancing my career.*

4. **Presents a poor appearance and negative image.** Dresses inappropriately for the interview – under-dresses or over-dresses for the position. He or she may need to learn some basic grooming habits, from haircut and style to makeup and nails.

5. **Expresses bad, negative, and corrosive attitudes.** Tends to be negative, overbearing, extremely aggressive, cynical, and opinionated to the extreme. Expresses intolerance and strong prejudices toward others. Complains a lot about everything and everybody. In Yiddish such chronic complainers are known as kvetchers. Indicates a possible caustic personality that will not fit in well with the company. Regardless of how talented this person may be, unless he works in a cell by himself, he'll probably be fired within two months for having a bad attitude that pollutes the office and harms morale.

6. **Engages in inappropriate and unexpected behaviors for an interview situation.** Shows off scars, tattoos, muscles, or pictures of family. Flirts with the interviewer. Possibly an exhibitionist who may also want to date the boss and harass co-workers!

7. **Appears somewhat incoherent and unfocused.** Tends to offer incomplete thoughts, loses focus, and jumps around to unrelated ideas. Hard to keep a focused conversation going. Incoherent thought processes indicate a possible attention deficit disorder (ADD) problem.

8. **Inarticulate.** Speaks poorly, from sound of voice and diction to grammar, vocalized pauses, and jargon. Uses lots of *"you know," "ah," "like," "okay,"* and *"well"* fillers. Expresses a class street language - *"cool," "damn," "man," "wow."* Not a good candidate for using the telephone or interacting with clients. Appears verbally illiterate. Writing is probably similar.

9. **Gives short and incomplete answers to questions.** Tends to respond to most questions with *"Yes," "No," "Maybe,"* or *"I'm not sure"* when the interviewer expects more in-depth answers. Appears shallow and indicates a lack of substance, initiative, interest, and enthusiasm.

10. **Lacks a sense of direction.** Appears to have no goals or apparent objectives. Just looking for a job and paycheck rather than pursuing a passion or cause.

11. **Appears ill or has a possible undisclosed medical condition.** Looks pale, glassy-eyed, gaunt, or yellow. Coughs, sneezes, and sounds terrible. Talks about his upcoming operation – within six weeks of starting the job! Suspects this person may have an illness or a drug or alcohol addiction.

12. **Volunteers personal information that normally would be illegal or inappropriate to ask.** Candidate makes interviewer feel uncomfortable by talking about religion, political affiliation, age, family, divorce, sexual orientation, and physical and mental health.

13. **Emits bad or irritating smells.** Reeks of excessive perfume, cologne, or shaving lotion - could kill mosquitos! Can smell smoke or alcohol on breath. Strong body odor indicates personal hygiene problems. Has bad breath throughout the interview, which gets cut short for an unexplained reason!

14. **Shows little enthusiasm, drive, or initiative.** Appears to be just looking for a job and a paycheck. Tends to be passive and indifferent. No evidence of being a self-starter who takes initiative and solves problems on his own. Not sure what motivates this person other than close supervision. Indeed, he'll require lots of supervision or the company will have an employee with lots of play-time on his hands, or the job will

expand to fill the time allotted. He'll become the "job guy" who always says *"I did my job just like you told me,"* but not much beyond what's assigned. Don't expect much from this person, who will probably be overpaid for what he produces.

15. **Lacks confidence and self-esteem.** Seems unsure of self, nervous, and ill at ease. Lacks decisiveness in making decisions. Communicates uncertainty with such comments as *"I don't know," "Maybe," "I'm not sure," "Hadn't really thought of that," "Interesting question," "I'll have to think about that,"* or redirects with the question, *"Well, what do you think?"*

16. **Appears too eager and hungry for the job.** Is overly enthusiastic, engages in extreme flattery, and appears suspiciously nervous. Early in the interview, before learning much about the company or job, makes such comments as *"I really like it here," "I need this job," "Is there overtime?," "What are you paying?," "How many vacation days do you give?"*

17. **Communicates dishonesty or deception.** Uses canned interview language, evades probing questions, and appears disingenuous. Looks like a tricky character who has things to hide and thus will probably be sneaky and deceptive on the job.

18. **Feels too smooth and superficial.** Dresses nicely, has a firm handshake and good eye contact, answers most questions okay, and appears enthusiastic - just like the books tell job seekers to do. When asked more substantive *"What if"* and behavior-based questions, or requested to give examples of specific accomplishments, the candidate seems to be caught off balance and stumbles with incomplete answers. Can't put one's finger on the problem, but the gut reaction is that this role-playing candidate is very superficial and will probably end up being the "dressed for success" and "coached for the interview" employee from hell!

19. **Appears evasive when asked about possible problems with background.** Gives elusive answers to red flag questions about frequent job changes, termination, and time gaps in work history. Such answers raise questions about the interviewee's honesty, credibility, sense of responsibility, and overall behavior. Indicates a possible negative behavior pattern that needs further investigation.

20. **Speaks negatively of previous employers and co-workers.** When asked why he left previous employers, usually responds by bad-mouthing them. Has little good to say about others who apparently were not as important as this candidate.

21. **Maintains poor eye contact.** At least in North America, eye contact is an indication of trustworthiness and attention. Individuals who fail to maintain an appropriate amount of eye contact are often judged as untrustworthy - have something to hide. Having too little or too much eye contact during the interview gives off mixed messages about what you are saying. Worst of all, it may make the interviewer feel uncomfortable in your presence.

22. **Offers a limp or overly firm handshake.** Interviewers often get two kinds of handshakes from candidates - the wimps and the bone-crushers. Your initial handshake may say something about your personality. Candidates offering a cold, wet, and limp handshake often come across as corpses! Bone-crushers may appear too aggressive.

23. **Shows little interest in the company.** Indicates he didn't do much research, since he knows little about the company and didn't have time to check out the company's extensive website. Asks this killer question: *"What do you do here?"* Goodbye, again!

24. Talks about salary and benefits early in the interview. Rather than try to learn more about the company and position as well as demonstrate his value, the candidate seems preoccupied with salary and benefits by talking about them within the first 15 minutes of the interview. Shows little interest in the job or employer beyond the compensation package. When the interviewee prematurely starts to talk about compensation, red flags go up again - this is a self-centered candidate who is not really interested in doing the job or advancing a career.

25. Is discourteous, ill-mannered, and disrespectful. Arrives for the interview a half hour late with no explanation or a phone call indicating a problem en route. Just sits and waits for the interviewer to ask questions. Picks up things on the interviewer's desk. Challenges the interviewer's ideas. Closes the interview without thanking the interviewer for the opportunity to interview for the job. Not even going to charm and etiquette school would help this candidate!

26. Tells inappropriate jokes and laughs a lot. Attempts at humor bomb - appears to be a smart aleck who likes to laugh at his own jokes. Comes across as an irritating clown who says stupid and silly things. Will need to frequently put this one out to pasture to keep him away from other employees who don't share such humor.

27. Talks too much. Can't answer a question without droning on and on with lots of irrelevant talk. Volunteers all kinds of information, including interesting but sensitive personal observations and gossip, the interviewer neither needs nor wants. Doesn't know when to shut up. Would probably waste a lot of valuable work time talking, talking, and talking and thus irritating other employees. Seems to need lots of social strokes through talk which he readily initiates.

28. **Appears needy and greedy.** Talks a lot about financial needs and compensation. When discussing salary, talks about his personal financial situation, including debts and planned future purchases, rather than what the job is worth and what value he will bring to the job. Seems to expect the employer is interested in supporting his lifestyle, which may be a combination of irresponsible financial behavior, failing to plan (including family planning), living beyond his pay grade, and having bad luck. This line of talk indicates he probably has debilitating financial problems that go far beyond the salary level of this job. Not interested in paying for his needs.

29. **Fails to talk about accomplishments.** Candidate concentrates on explaining work history as primarily consisting of assigned duties and responsibilities. When asked to give examples of his five major accomplishments in his last jobs, doesn't seem to understand the question, gives little evidence of performance, or reverts once again to discussing formal duties and responsibilities. When probed further for accomplishments, can't really say much and shows discomfort about this line of questioning.

30. **Does not ask questions about the job or employer.** When asked *"Do you have any questions?,"* replies *"No"* or *"You've covered everything."* Asking questions is often more important than answering questions. When you ask thoughtful questions, you emphasize your interest in the employer and job as well as indicate your intelligence - qualities employers look for in candidates.

31. **Appears self-centered rather than employer-centered.** This will become immediately apparent by the direction of the answers and questions coming from the interviewee. If they primarily focus on benefits to the interviewee, the candidate

will tend to be self-centered. For example, a candidate who frequently uses "I" when talking about himself and the job may be very self-centered. On the other hand, the candidate who talks about "we" and "you" is usually more employer-oriented. Contrast these paired statements about the job and compensation:

> *"What would I be doing in this position?"*
> *"What do you see us achieving over the next six months?"*
>   or
> *"What would I be making on this job?"*
> *"What do you normally pay for someone with my qualifications?"*

32. **Demonstrates poor listening skills.** Doesn't listen carefully to questions or seems to have her own agenda that overrides the interviewer's interest. Tends to go off in different directions from the questions being asked. Not a very empathetic listener both verbally and nonverbally. Seems to be more interested in doing the talking than focusing on the issues at hand. Apparently wants to take charge of the interview and be the Lone Ranger. The job really does require good listening skills!

33. **Seems not too bright for the job.** Answering simple interview questions is like taking an intelligence test. Has difficulty talking about past accomplishments. Doesn't seem to grasp what the job is all about or the skills required. Seems confused and lacks focus. Should never have gotten to the job interview but had a terrific looking resume which was probably written by a professional resume writer for $300!

34. **Fails to properly prepare for the interview.** This is the most important mistake of all. It affects all the other mistakes. Indeed, failing to prepare will immediately show when the can-

didate makes a bad first impression, fails to indicate knowledge about the company and job, gives poor answers to standard interview questions, and does not ask questions. In other words, the candidate makes many of the mistakes outlined above because he or she failed to anticipate what goes into a winning interview. Since you should be communicating your very best self during the interview, failing to prepare for it says something about how you deal with important things in your life and work. In this case, the employer and job were not important enough for you to prepare properly. That's okay. The employer now knows the real serious you.

35. **Closes the interview by just leaving.** How you close the interview may determine whether or not you will be invited back to another interview or offered the job. Most interviewees fail to properly close interviews, as we will discuss in Chapter 10. At the very least, you need to summarize the interview, indicate continuing interest in the position, thank the interviewer for the opportunity to meet, ask when a hiring decision might be made, and ask for permission to call the interviewer within a week to learn about your status.

9

Challenging Questions and Sample Answers

I N MOST INSTANCES YOU can accurately predict 95 percent or more of the interview questions you will be asked.
Most, perhaps all, of these questions will be similar to the
questions outlined in this chapter. As you anticipate how
you would respond if you encounter each of these questions in an
interview, remember that you are formulating your strategy for a
response. You should not try to determine the exact words you
would use and then memorize them. To do this would be a big
mistake. At best, your answer would likely sound memorized and
you would greatly diminish your credibility. At worst, you might
forget your memorized response in the middle of your answer!

So consider your answers in terms of basic strategies. What do you hope to convey as you respond to each question? Your goal is to convince the interviewer that you should be offered the job. So, as you respond, think in terms of the needs of the employer. How do your goals fit with their business needs? Keep this basic tenet in mind as you formulate your strategies in responding to questions you are asked. Try to make time prior to the interview to actually talk through your answers to questions. You may practice answering interview questions (which you have made into a list) posed by a friend or family member, or you can read each question and then respond. Practice talking your answers into a tape recorder. Play back the tape and evaluate how you sound.

> *Memorized answers to questions will sound memorized and thus greatly diminish your credibility.*

- Do you exude confidence?
- Do you sound dynamic?
- Do you talk in a conversational style (rather than your response sounding like a "canned" answer)?
- Do you speak without excessive fillers such as *"ah," "and ah," "like,"* and *"you know"*?
- Do you seem authentic and believable?
- Do you appear likable?

101 Questions You May Be Asked

We examine strategies and specific answers to most of the following 101 questions in our companion interview book, ***Nail the Job Interview: 101 Dynamite Answers to Interview Questions*** (Impact Publications, 2003). While we're mainly concerned about answering red flag questions in this book, which appear in the second half of this chapter, it's useful to first review the different types of general questions you may be asked as you prepare for your job interview. Some of these questions may be phrased differently during an actual job interview. Try to give your best response to each question using a tape recorder. Then listen to your recorded responses and critique them.

Each time you talk through an answer, your words will be somewhat different since you have purposely not tried to memorize your response. You have thought through the strategy of your response, the gist of the message you want to convey, but you have not attempted to commit a response to memory. Interview questions tend to fall into five major categories. Let's briefly summarize these questions as follows:

Questions Related to Your Personality and Motivation

1. Why should we hire you?
2. Are you a self-starter?
3. What is your greatest strength?
4. What is your greatest weakness?
5. What would you most like to improve about yourself?
6. What are some of the reasons for your success?
7. Describe your typical workday.
8. Do you anticipate problems or do you react to them?
9. How do you deal with stressful situations?
10. Do you ever lose your temper?
11. How well do you work under deadlines?
12. What contributions did you make to your last company?
13. What will you bring to this position that others won't?
14. How well do you get along with your superiors?
15. How well do you get along with your co-workers?
16. How do you manage your subordinates?
17. How do you feel about working with superiors who may have less education than you?

18. Do you prefer working alone or with others?
19. How do others view your work?
20. How do you deal with criticism?
21. Do you consider yourself to be someone who takes greater initiative than others?
22. Do you consider yourself a risk-taker?
23. Are you a good time manager?
24. How important is job security?
25. How do you define success?
26. How do you spend your leisure time?
27. What would be the perfect job for you?
28. What really motivates you to perform on the job?
29. How well do you work with clients?
30. How do you deal with competing demands?
31. Have you ever had to lie for someone on the job?
32. Have you ever wanted to quit a job?
33. Have you ever wanted to fire your boss?

Questions Related to Your
Education and Training

34. Why didn't you graduate from high school?
35. Why didn't you go to college?
36. Why didn't you finish college?
37. Why did you select college?
38. Why did you major in _____ ?
39. What was your minor in school?
40. How did your major relate to the work you have done since graduation?
41. Why weren't your grades better in school?
42. What subjects did you enjoy most?
43. What subjects did you enjoy least?
44. If you could go back and do it over again, what would you change about your education?

45. What extracurricular school activities did you participate in?
46. Tell me about your role in [an extracurricular activity].
47. What leadership positions did you hold?
48. How does your degree prepare you for the job at _____?
49. Did you have a job while you were in school?
50. Are you planning to take additional courses or start graduate school over the next year or two?
51. If you had a choice of several short training sessions to attend, which two or three would you select?
52. What materials do you read regularly to keep up with what is going on in your field?
53. What is the most recent skill you have learned?
54. What are your educational goals over the next few years?

Questions Related to Your Experience and Skills

55. Why do you want to leave your job?
56. Why have you changed jobs so frequently?
57. Why would you be more likely to stay here?
58. What are your qualifications for this job?
59. What experience prepares you for this job?
60. What did you like most about your present/ most recent job?
61. What did you like least about that job?
62. What did you like most about your boss?
63. What did you like least about that boss?
64. Tell me about an ongoing responsibility in your current/ most recent job that you enjoyed.
65. How does your present/most recent job relate to the overall goals of your department/the company?
66. What has your present/most recent supervisor(s) criticized about your work?

67. What duties in your present/most recent job do you find it difficult to do?

68. Why do you want to leave your present job? Are you being forced out?

69. Why should we hire someone like you, with your experience and motivation?

70. What type of person would you hire for this position?

71. Have you ever been fired or asked to resign?

72. What was the most important contribution you made on your last job?

73. What do you wish you had accomplished in your present/most recent job but were unable to?

74. What is the most important thing you've learned from the jobs you've held?

Questions About Your Career Goals

75. Tell me about yourself.

76. Tell me about your career goals.

77. What would you like to accomplish during the next five years [or ten years]?

78. How do your career goals today differ from your career goals five years ago?

79. Where do you see yourself five years from now?

80. Describe a major goal you set for yourself recently?

81. What are you doing to achieve that goal?

82. Have you ever thought of switching careers?

83. How does this job compare to what would be the perfect job for you?

84. What would you change about our company to make this your ideal workplace?

85. How long have you been looking for another job?

Questions Related to Why You Want This Job

86. What do you know about our company?
87. What trends do you see in our industry?
88. Why do you want to work for us?
89. How much business would you bring to our company?
90. What similarities do you see between this and your current/most recent position?
91. What makes this position different from your current/most recent position?
92. Why are you willing to take a job you are over-qualified for?
93. Why are you willing to take a pay cut from your previous [present] position?
94. What would you change about this position?
95. How long would you expect to stay with our company?
96. How do you feel about working overtime or on weekends?
97. Are you willing to relocate?
98. How much are you willing to travel?
99. What are your salary requirements?
100. How soon could you begin work?
101. Do you have any questions?

Unexpected and Wacky Questions

You may not be asked any questions beyond the ones outlined in this book. If the questions you are asked do go beyond these, they will most likely fall into one of three categories:

- Specific questions that relate to special knowledge or skills required for the job for which you are being considered.

- Questions that are raised by unusual items or unexplained gaps or omissions on your resume or application.

- Questions to catch you off guard and/or test your thought processes, such as *"If you could choose to be any fish in the water, which one would you be? Why?"*

Be sure to look over your resume for possible questions the employer might ask you. Is there anything that stands out? If you spent some time abroad, the interviewer may be curious about your experiences as well as what your living and/or working abroad choices say about you. If you have a two-year unexplained gap in your job history, this gap is bound to raise the question of what you were doing during this time. As we will discuss later in this chapter, you need to be ready with honest, yet positive, answers that will further promote your candidacy rather than knock you out of the running.

> *You need to be ready with honest, yet positive, answers that will promote your candidacy.*

If you have thoughtfully considered your responses and practiced responding with the gist of the message you want to convey, these questions should not throw you. However, if you haven't given such questions much thought, your responses are likely to show it.

Few questions should ever be answered with just a *"yes"* or *"no."* Remember to provide **examples** as often as possible to support the points you make. If asked by the interviewer whether you are a self-starter you could simply respond *"yes."* However, you will score few points for this monosyllabic response. It really says nothing except either that you think you are a self-starter or you think this is the response the interviewer wants to hear. But if you follow your *"yes"* response with an example or two of what you did that demonstrates you were a self-starter in your last job (or in school if you have just graduated and have little work experience), you start to sell yourself. You want to impress the interviewer and you want to stand out from the rest of the applicants being interviewed.

Remember to use examples and use them frequently. The examples you use to support the assertions you make help to sell "you" to the interviewer. Examples make what you say about your skills and achievements more clear, more interesting, more credible, and more likely to be remembered.

Behavior- and Situation-Based Questions

Employers are increasingly incorporating behavior-based and situation-based questions in job interviews. **Behavior-based** questions arise when the interviewer asks you to describe how you responded when you faced an actual situation.

These questions get interviewees to do what they are supposed to do – think on their feet and give rich examples.

Hypothetical situational-based questions don't ask for an actual situation, but require you to consider a possible situation and describe how you would act if that occurred. Difficult to prepare for, these types of interview questions are an attempt to get applicants to do what they should be doing anyway: think on their feet and expand their answers with rich examples that support the assertions they are making.

Be prepared to respond to these types of open-ended behavior-based and situation-based questions:

1. What would you do if . . .
2. In what situations have you become so involved in the work you were doing that the day flew by?
3. If you were to encounter that same situation now, how would you deal with that person?
4. If you had a choice of working in our department A or department B, which would you choose?

5. Why would you make that choice?

6. Tell me about a recent time when you took responsibility for a task that was outside of your job description.

7. Tell me about a time when you took action without your supervisor's prior approval.

Red Flag Questions and Issues

If you have any red flags in your background, such as those outlined in Chapter 2, be prepared to handle questions related to them. Here are some useful strategies related to sample questions and answers for dealing with such red flag issues.

No Experience

If the interviewer starts asking questions about your work experience, he might note the following:

> *"I see from your resume that you have no experience working in the landscape business. We normally hire candidates with at least one year experience. Can you tell me a little more about your experience and how it relates to this position?"*

Don't let this objection deter you from selling yourself for the position. Experience is a very relative term, and it relates to many different types of skills acquired in different settings, ranging from work to play. For example, have you worked in any volunteer positions? Did you have an internship? Don't limit your thinking to formal jobs or ones you were paid to do. If, for example, you had your own small business mowing lawns and doing yard work or if you had a paper route, you can draw on these experiences as you talk about skills you acquired, things you accomplished, and valuable experiences that prepared you for the job in question. What skills did you use in many of your life experiences?

- Interacted with clients
- Showed up when expected and on time

- Worked well with team members
- Managed time, doing hardest tasks first
- Was so successful I had to bring on a partner to help with all the business generated

Your life probably doesn't mirror this hypothetical example, but if you think hard enough, you may find you have some experiences you can use to bolster your work experience that you can talk about.

Someone following this strategy might respond to the above "lack of experience in landscaping" question by stating the following:

"I'm sure this is a concern since I've not previously worked for a landscape company. But let me explain where I'm coming from and why I feel I'm well suited for this position. In my previous job as well as in most tasks I undertake - be it a member of the Ravens baseball team, assistant to our church youth group, or chairman of the road maintenance committee of our community association - I'm a quick learner who understands the importance of getting things done in a well organized and timely manner. I'm a hard worker who enjoys contributing to the success of others. I believe I have the necessary experience, skills, and qualities to become a very productive member of your team. I've done lots of part-time yard work and even designed the patio and selected plants for my neighbor's back yard. I brought some pictures to show you what I did using a combination of flowering trees, scrubs, and flag stone. I love this type of work. I can assure you that my interests, attitude, enthusiasm, and drive will more than make up for my lack of formal work experience."

Poor Grades

If an employer knows you had poor grades in school, he will most likely interpret that as a sign of failure or weakness. He may or may not follow up with a question about your educational performance. Whether he asks this question or not, it will most likely be on his mind and you need to address it:

"C's, D's, and F's? Why didn't you do better in school?"

Don't let this question go by without dealing with it head on. For example, did you just goof off and not take school seriously? If so, it's probably best you own up to it, accept responsibility, and indicate what an immature attitude you had at the time. If you have been in any training classes since, and you have a better record of performance, then bring that into the discussion as an indication of your maturity. On the other hand, perhaps you had extenuating circumstances, such as working 25 hours a week while going to school. Or perhaps you had a learning disorder (dyslexia, ADD, or ADHD) which was finally diagnosed, treated, and overcome. Recognizing that you had this problem and dealt with it will be a real plus in the eyes of most employers who appreciate confessions and stories about self-improvement. An example of a good response to the "poor grades" question would be this:

> *"My performance in school was one of those more embarrassing periods in my life. As a kid I was very immature. I really didn't have much interest in school. I also ran around with the wrong crowd. While I could have done much better had I been more focused on learning, I did just enough to get by and have a good time with my buddies. After graduating, I spent a couple of years going from one job to another. That was a real wake-up call about my future. After two years, I decided it was time to do something else with my life. And that's when I came back to education. I wanted to go to college to study criminal justice and security, but my high school grades were too bad to get into most places. I also couldn't afford the costs, and I didn't qualify for most student loans. So I decided to take a few classes at the community college, where I could get in as well as afford the tuition. My first semester was really tough - I had to learn how to learn. But I got through with three B's - the most I had ever gotten in school! This semester I'm really enjoying my English and Computer Science classes. While it may take me several years to finish my degree while I work full time, I'm determined to do so. Education and learning have become very important to me. I now have clearer goals and better skills which I can put to use in the security field. I just hope employers will look at what I've done since high school and my poor high school performance won't hold me back."*

No Diploma

If you dropped out of high school, expect the employer to take notice and raise the obvious question:

"Why didn't you complete high school? What happened?"

After all, most people in today's workforce are expected to graduate from high school and many go on to college. People who don't graduate from high school stand out from the crowd - they are suspected of carrying some troubling baggage and may be viewed as damaged goods. High school drop-outs are generally seen as losers.

If this question relates to you, make sure you're prepared with a good answer. What was your reason for dropping out of school? Did you make a mistake and are now trying to correct it? Did you have extenuating circumstances, from family to health issues? Certainly some reasons are better than others, but the bottom line is this: What are you doing or going to do about it now? Are you working on your GED? If not, why not? Having a GED or evidence that you are working on getting it suggests you are a purposeful and motivated individual.

One example of a response to this question is this:

"I'm not stupid, but I did have lots of problems in high school. I guess I was what many call a 'juvenile delinquent'. I was constantly in trouble with my parents, teachers, and local authorities. Since my attendance was so poor and I created problems for the school, I was repeatedly expelled. In fact, one teacher told me I would never amount to anything. That really made me mad - perhaps it was my wake-up call. I never forgot what she said, and I wanted to prove her wrong. After dropping out of school, I ended up in a lot of minimum wage jobs that literally confirmed what my parents and teachers had been telling me for years - get a good education and follow your dreams. Well, being 20 years old without a high school diploma and few skills is a tough road to travel. At 20 I remembered that teacher's comment about not amounting to anything. She was right - I was headed down a very predictable road of failure. One day I literally woke up and said 'I've made a lot of mistakes but I'm going to be somebody'. So the first thing I did was visit that teacher and ask for her help. She was great. She advised me to quickly get my GED. I immediately enrolled in a class and successfully completed my GED in June. It was a great day - I felt I had put my life back on track. Now I want to take some college courses, especially related to computer science. I love computers, and I can't wait to learn more about this fascinating field. That's why I'm so interested in this job."

Were Fired

As soon as an employer knows you have been fired, he or she is curious about why it happened:

"Why were you fired from your last job?"

"Have you been fired from other jobs?"

If you've been fired from more than one job, the employer will be concerned about a possible pattern of behavior that could be repeated in his company. No one wants to hire someone who is likely to become a problem employee requiring termination. On the other hand, being fired is not necessarily a problem. People get fired every day for all types of reasons, from routine personnel changes to serious violations of workplace rules. If the reason relates to unacceptable behavior, be sure you have a truthful and credible story indicating the problem has been dealt with and no longer exists. What was the situation? Put the best honest spin on it that you can; take responsibility for whatever negative behaviors are rightfully yours; and indicate what you have learned from the experience. Whatever you do, don't bad-mouth your former employer or put the blame on others.

A good example of a response to the firing question is this:

"I was let go at L. C. Construction Company because of my spotty attendance record. I was supposed to arrive at the work site at 6:30am. However, I often came in at 7am or 8am and sometimes as late as 1pm. Some days I didn't show up altogether, and occasionally I would disappear for two or three days without informing my supervisor. He warned me twice about my erratic behavior. Jobs weren't getting done because I couldn't be relied upon. The last time I literally disappeared for a week without contacting my supervisor. When I did finally show up, he told me my services were no longer needed and told me to clean out my locker. In fact, when I look back, I'm surprised he didn't fire me earlier. I haven't told anyone this story because it's still embarrassing. But here is what was really happening to me and those around me. I was going through a very difficult period in my life. I had a serious drug and alcohol abuse problem that nearly destroyed me and my family. I didn't face up to it until I got fired. The day I got fired was also the day my wife left me and moved in with her mother. She told me it was over unless I got some profes-

sional help. I had hit rock bottom and I was extremely depressed as my life fell apart. So I called my minister for counsel. He recommended that we pray together and then contact community services about a very good drug and alcohol abuse program offered through the county hospital. I just couldn't pick up the phone and make that call. I guess it meant admitting my failures and taking responsibility. He said don't worry - he would make the call and set up an appointment. What a lifesaver! This was the best thing that had happened to me in a long time. I literally surrendered to the program on the first day and religiously followed everything I was told was necessary to get rid of the demons that were controlling my life. Indeed, I got some excellent one-on-one counseling and joined a life-changing support group. I discovered I wasn't alone. I also learned how to take better control of my life by setting goals and following some basic time management skills. Within a couple of months I had kicked my habits and started putting my life back together. I have been doing volunteer construction work during the past two months with the Community Building Project for low income families. I haven't missed a day of work there, and I'm really making a difference in the lives of people, many who have gone through similar problems to those I encountered. Best of all, I'm back with my family and we have dreams for a new future. I also enrolled in a new home inspection program at our local community college. I should get my CRT certification by December. I can honestly say I've literally changed my life. If you hire me, you won't be inheriting my old self. While I'm now clean, I'm still part of a 12-step program, which I will continue participating in because it has been such a great support group. It keeps me focused on taking responsibility and setting and achieving realistic goals, and it continues to remind me that this is a life-long challenge that I have to continue working at. I'm excited about the possibility of joining your company as an apprentice building inspector – always on time, dependable, and focused on results."

Job Hopper

Employers want employees who intend to stay with them for a reasonable length of time - at least two years but ideally five years or more. While they don't expect you to be with them a lifetime, neither do they want to spend time and money training you for your next employer. If you have a history of frequent job changes, chances are employers will view you as a potential job hopper who will most likely become a high cost liability for the company. On the other hand, some positions tend to be high turnover positions, especially in sales, restaurants, hospitality, entertainment, construction, and seasonal industries. In fact, many restaurants experience nearly a 100 percent turnover of personnel in a single year! While it's often easy to find employment in industries that have high turnover rates, it's also easy to lose a job in such industries and thus appear to be a job hopper.

> *Employers don't want to spend time and money training you for your next employer.*

The appearance of being a job hopper usually shows up on paper - on your resume or application, which includes listing your employment history. Organized chronologically, your work history indicates a pattern of behavior. If you have a history of frequent job changes, the interviewer will most likely ask you this potential knock-out question:

> *"I see from your application that you've worked for four employers during the past five years. That concerns me since our average employee has been with us for 3½ years. Why did you change jobs so often?"*

This question might be followed up with another obvious question:

> *"If we offer you this job, how long do you expect to stay with our company?"*

> *"What do you see as being different here that would cause you to stay three to five years?"*

Think carefully before you answer these questions. What were the situations? Were you fired, your company downsized, you lost interest, advanced your career, took short-term or temporary jobs for financial reasons, or worked in a high turnover industry? Whatever your situation or reasons, try to put the best face on it you honestly can and take responsibility. Here's a possible positive response to the initial question:

> *"I know four employers in five years may raise a red flag about my willingness to stay with an employer. But let me explain what happened. My first two jobs as a waiter had nothing to do with my career interests or long-term plans. They*

were really temporary jobs that helped me financially get through a two-year certification program in telecommunications. Upon completing the program, I landed a job with a telecommunications firm. Unfortunately, and to everyone's surprise, that company went out of business within six months. I then moved to another telecommunications firm which also went out of business within a year. I had no idea how volatile the telecommunications field was when I started school. In fact, this was one of the hottest fields around a few years ago and then the bubble burst right at the time I started my new career. I'm looking for a stable employer, such as you, who plans to be in business for a long time and who values your employees. That's what attracted me to your company. I've heard many good things about it being one of the best companies for work for in this region. I would expect to stay with you as long as possible. I see this as a place where I can grow professionally with a long and productive career working with a very exciting group of people. Given my last two jobs with companies that closed, I do have a few questions about this company and its future."

There are many other possible scenarios relating to job hopping concerns. If you indeed are a serial job hopper who has difficulty staying with an employer for a reasonable period of time, you'll need to convince this employer that you are now different; your pattern of behavior has changed. Give examples of what you have done, as well as what you intend to do, that will make a difference. But if you look like a job hopper because you were fired from your last four jobs, you are well advised to seek professional help in dealing with what may well be some serious personal- and work-related issues.

No Focus to Jobs Held

Employers also look for candidates who seem to have a sense of purpose. They know what they want to do, set career goals, and follow through. Most employers can "read between the lines" when reviewing a candidate's work history. One thing they often look for is a pattern of career advancement. If your resume or application shows a hodge-podge of jobs held in a variety of areas and a job change did not usually result in a step up the career ladder, you have a red flag that needs careful attention. You may be asked this type of knock-out question:

"I noticed on your resume that you've had seven jobs during the past ten years. But they seem to be all over the place - from a cook and car salesman to repairman and security guard. Few of these jobs seem to relate to this supervisory position at our day-care center. Can you elaborate on your work history and how it relates to what we do here?"

As you prepare for such a question, explain your situation, focus on some common elements that tie together these jobs, and note what has possibly changed in your life that has now given you renewed career direction. Here's an example of a possible response to the question:

"I'm glad you asked that question since it's very important that my employer understand where I'm coming from and going in the future. You're right about my background and it obviously shows. For too long I didn't know what I really wanted to do. I always seemed to be getting new work experience but little career satisfaction. After this last job, I decided it was time to do something different about my life. So I went to see a career counselor, Janet Howard, at the local One-Stop Career Center. Did I ever get an eye-opening! The first thing she asked was 'What do you want to do with the rest of your life?' I couldn't answer that question. I knew what I didn't want to do, which was what I had been doing. The next thing she did was to have me take a series of career-related tests, including the Myers-Briggs Type Indicator and Strong Interest Inventory. Based on those results, I next took a few aptitude tests and explored various career options. I then developed a detailed career plan, including what I really wanted to do over the next ten years. I now look back at my various jobs and wish I had met Ms. Howard ten years earlier! However, I also learned that I did gain some valuable experience in those jobs that do directly relate to my career plans. In particular, I often supervised people and really enjoyed this aspect of these jobs. Since I also love kids, I couldn't think of a better job to launch my new career. By the way, I didn't put Ms. Howard down as one of my references, but you may want to talk to her about my testing results. She knows a great deal about my skills, interests, and aptitudes that would be relevant to this job."

Poor References

Expect to be asked for references and expect employers to contact your previous employers for information about you. If you have some skeletons in the closet with previous employers, it's time you take some important actions to ensure that they do not become killer references.

Since references are normally checked between the period you are interviewed and offered the job, you may never have a chance to address any red flag questions arising from what your references say about you. Therefore, it's extremely important that you choose your references well so that no unexpected red flags get tossed your way during this critical decision-making phase. Think hard and try to identify some people who will give you a good reference (other than your relatives!). By carefully selecting, you may be able to salvage this one.

Try to select references that fall into the following categories:

- **Former employers:** Can verify your work history and talk about your accomplishments and pattern of work behavior. If you have former employers who may speak ill of you, heed our advice at the end of this section.

- **Character witness:** An associate, minister, or someone else whom you have worked with who can speak about your good character.

If you have a difficult background and you know the employer knows this, include a reference who can testify to how you have turned your life around. If, for example, you were recently incarcerated and appear rehabilitated, this person might be a prison minister, chief psychologist, education officer, or parole officer - not a former inmate.

When you go to the job interview, make sure you have a list of references to give to the interviewer. If they don't appear on your application, the interviewer will most likely ask for your references during the interview. Consequently, it's always a good idea to contact your references before sharing them with an employer. Let your potential references know you are conducting a job search and ask for their permission to serve as a reference. Give them a copy of your resume, or a summary of your background, and tell them they may be called by a few employers who will be checking you out. Go one step further and ask if they could serve as a favorable reference. The more information you give them about yourself and how you fit the position in question, the better prepared they will be to give you a good reference.

Let's talk about one type of reference you might want to avoid because he or she could be potentially damaging to your future - a former employer who fired you or one you left in a huff. In fact, the interviewer may ask you if it's okay for her to contact your former employer. If you say "no," you raise a red flag. Be ready to say "yes" to such requests. This may be the time to mend some old broken fences. If you left a position under difficult circumstances, it may be to your benefit to make up with your former employer. Turn any anger into forgiveness. Call him and make amends for any ill feelings. Time has passed, both you and he have changed, and it's time to get on with your life. Chances are he will be receptive to this gesture. Tell him what you have been doing since you left, what changes have taken place, and ask if he will be willing to serve as a favorable reference. Regardless of the circumstances of your leaving this employer, in the end most employers wish their former employees the best, even though they might never hire them again. They understand the culture of references - stress the positives and overlook the negatives. After all, we all need to get on with our lives. In fact, he may become one of your strongest supporters in the reference department!

Ex-Offender

Statistics tell an important, sobering, and often whispered story. People with criminal backgrounds have some of the brightest red flags flying. In the United States over 2 million people are currently incarcerated; 600,000 people are annually released on probation; nearly 5 million people remain on parole or probation; and over 30 million people have some type of conviction on their record. While not widely publicized, a large percentage of local government employment programs (Workforce Development) are aimed at helping ex-offenders transition to the world of work. Baltimore, Maryland, for example, alone absorbs over up to 10,000 ex-offenders each year. Ex-offenders present special challenges for career counselors, who must deal with many types of red flag behaviors, ranging from murder to assault. And many ex-offenders become known as local sex offenders with limited employment opportunities.

> *Employers want to hire <u>rehabilitated ex-offenders</u> who take responsibility and do not pose problems for the employer and fellow employees.*

That's millions of red flags waving in front of employers! So why would an employer want to hire someone with a criminal background? The answer is simple: Thousands of employers hire ex-offenders each day because they have desirable skills and work habits; many also work for very low wages. But they want to hire rehabilitated ex-offenders who take responsibility and do not pose problems for the employer and fellow employees.

The first knock-out question most ex-offenders face often appears on an application form or in the job interview:

"Have you ever been convicted of a felony? If yes, give details."

If you have convicted, how should you best respond to this question on an application form? You basically have four choices:

1. Lie by saying *"no."*

2. Don't respond - just leave it blank and go on to another question.

3. Be truthful by saying *"yes"* and give the details.

4. Be truthful by saying *"yes"* and then follow up by saying *"details provided at the interview."*

Whatever you do, don't lie. Lying will just delay the inevitable - the employer will most likely find out about your conviction during a background check. Leaving the question unanswered implies you may have something to hide, although your non-response to this question may be overlooked and the question may never again be raised. Writing about the details gives you little opportunity to explain what happened and what changes have taken place since your conviction. Your best course of action would be to inform the employer that you will provide details at the interview. You want to do this because you need to be in control of the story relating to your conviction.

Once you get to the interview, the interviewer may ask about your conviction. This is the time to do two things:

1. **Take responsibility for your actions.** Whatever you do, don't retry your case, blame your problems on others, and talk on and on about the problem. Your listener is not really interested in learning all the details, which may be scary to some people who are not used to dealing with ex-offenders. Give a very brief overview of what happened to you - the crime, the conviction, the outcome. You should be able to do this within one minute.

2. **Focus on how you have changed your life for the better because of this experience.** Remember, the employer wants to hire your future - not your past. Let him know that you are a mature, trustworthy, and loyal individual who has the requisite motivation, attitudes, and skills to do the job in question. You've learned important life lessons. Now you want to get on with a new and productive life. You only ask that the employer give you a chance to earn his trust and prove your value. This part of your story may take three to five minutes. But again, don't talk too much - just enough to let the employer know you are a new and potentially very productive person.

Employers are like many other people - sympathetic to individuals who have made mistakes but who are willing to take responsibility and make sincere efforts to change their lives. It's part of our culture of forgiveness, redemption, and self-transformation. After all, we all make mistakes, although some are more egregious errors than others. We all want to believe in the power of self-transformation - the ability to break out of self-destructive patterns of behavior and create a new life based upon

> *We live in a culture of forgiveness, redemption, and self-transformation.*

new attitudes, motivations, and goals. Whatever you do, make sure you stress your future rather than dwell on your past. Again, employers want to hire your future, despite your past.

Here's an instructive example of an ex-offender's response to the conviction question:

"Yes, I had problems when I was 18. I was convicted of car theft and drug possession. At the time I was a high school dropout, unemployed, and ran around with the wrong crowd. Needless to say, I was very immature and stupid. I pled guilty and was given a 10-year sentence at Morain Correctional Institution. Within a few weeks I knew I had hit rock bottom. I was surprised how many fellow inmates were repeat offenders - their whole life was just talking big, getting into more trouble, and doing more time. The stuff that went on there was scary. I didn't want to be a part of that group. By chance I had an opportunity to work in the library. For the first time in my life I was surrounded by a forest of books. While I did not finish school, I was a good reader. Those books soon became my best new friends. In the library one day I picked up a book entitled 'Your Purpose in Life'. Wow! It literally changed my life. Indeed, I was determined to change my life and never again come in contact with the criminal justice system. I wanted to be out for good and to dream dreams I never had. The first thing I did was to share my thoughts with the librarian who had taken special interest in me. She suggested I get my GED and then she recommended a good reading list to help me better plan my life, from inspirational books to materials on alternative careers for people without a four-year degree. Within a year I got my GED and then enrolled in the prison college program where I soon discovered I had a good aptitude for electrical engineering. I couldn't believe how much I loved learning. This opened a whole new world to me. With the help of my teachers, the chief

psychologist, and the librarian - and my parents who stood by me doing this difficult period in my life - I was able to turn what appeared to be a very bad situation, incarceration, into one of the best things that ever happened to me. Within three years I was released on good behavior. I've definitely matured. I have a wonderful girl friend who is a teacher, and I'm continuing to take courses at the community college. I hope to complete my Associate Degree in Electrical Engineering within the next three years. I'm very excited about eventually becoming an electrical engineering technician with your company. Right now I'm looking at my future, but I'm also well aware that I have some baggage that will be with me the rest of my life. I'm just hoping that employers will look at what I've done with my life during the past three years rather than when I was 18 and give me a chance to prove that I will become one of their most valuable employees."

But let's also acknowledge that some criminal activities are difficult to deal with in the job market. For example, if you have been convicted of assault, murder, or a sex crime, your red flag is bigger than most red flags of ex-offenders. These are frightening crimes for many employers who do not want the liability of such individuals working next to other employees. If you've done time for such crimes, you'll need to put together a rehabilitation portfolio as well as seek jobs with employers who are known to work with such ex-offenders.

Abused Drugs or Alcohol

No one wants to hire someone with a drug or alcohol abuse problem. After all, these problems plague many companies, which already spend millions of dollars each year on employee assistance programs designed to rehabilitate workers who abuse substances, and hence themselves. Many companies now require drug testing as a condition of employment. If you've ever walked into a Home Depot, you'll even see a sign posted at the entry for would-be applicants: "We require drug tests of all candidates." If you have a drug or alcohol problem, chances are you also have other problems that are best treated with professional help.

Most employers will not ask you about your drug and alcohol practices. Instead, they will see if you are drug free when they send you off for a drug test. However, drug and alcohol abuse problems tend to manifest themselves in other behavior problems related to the workplace - erratic work habits, low performance, excessive sick days, lack of focus, frequent job changes, and being fired. A good example of how to deal with this issue was covered in the earlier example under "Were Fired." Again, your best strategy is to come clean by taking responsibility and explaining what you have done to change your life so that substance abuse is no longer a problem for you and an employer in the workplace. Forgiveness, redemption, and self-transformation apply equally to this red flag issue as they do to many issues related to ex-offenders.

Over-Qualified

Many employers receive resumes and applications from individuals who appear over-qualified for the position being filled. Some are tempted to interview such individuals simply because they have much to offer given the level of the position. But such employers also must be realistic. Someone who appears over-qualified for the position will most likely be a problem employee. The person may not be happy working beneath his or her skill and pay level. As a result, the person may quickly leave when a better opportunity comes along. Such people may also be hiding an employment problem, such as being fired. On a more positive note, the individual may be in the process of changing careers and thus what initially appears as over-qualifications may be nothing more than an attempt to start a new career involving a new set of interests and skills. Indeed, it's not unusual for individuals to change careers two to three times during their worklife.

Whatever the case, the employer may raise this potential red flag question:

"You have an impressive resume. But one thing really concerns me. You appear over-qualified for this position. Why are you particularly interested in an entry-level production job when you have such an extensive managerial background?"

In reading between the lines, the interviewer is really raising an objection to hiring you: You won't be happy here and you won't stay long. Knowing this, your strategy should be to alleviate any doubts in the interviewer's mind that you really want this job. Be truthful, transparent, and enthusiastic. An example of an excellent response to this question is this:

> *"You're right. I do appear over-qualified for this position. In fact, I had a real problem writing a resume that indicated what I really wanted to do next in my life. My resume shouts 'Manager'. Given my more than 20 years of progressive management experience, it would appear I would be looking for a $100,000+ a year senior management position. But that's not what I really want to do in the future. Over the years I enjoyed the work and accomplished a lot in various management positions. During the last six months I began reassessing what I really wanted to do with the rest of my life. The answer was not to become another manager. I've been there, done that. Now I want to do something more personally and professionally rewarding. And money is no longer a major concern - the kids have graduated from college and we recently paid off the house mortgage. I now feel comfortable changing careers. I want to do something more creative and in line with my artistic interests. In fact, for many years I've had a wonderful and fascinating hobby - photography. I've taken numerous photos and even won an award in a travel magazine last year for a monastery shot I took on a photo tour to Bhutan two years ago. Recently I've moved into digital photography, which opened a whole new world of creative work. I brought my portfolio with me to show you samples of my work. I simply want to become a well respected professional photographer. I don't want to manage anyone or anything - just take great photos and contribute to the success of your studio. I also would be happy to share any of my management experience with you should it be relevant to this company. Could I show you my portfolio? I'm sure it won't make me look over-qualified, but I think it will tell you my story better than my resume."*

Questions You Should Ask

One of the most important questions you can answer is that last one on our list of 101 questions - *"Do you have any questions?"* The answer should be *"Yes, I have a few questions."* No matter how thorough the interview, no matter how much give-and-take, you should have at least two or three questions to ask near the end of the interview. Not asking any questions may hurt your chances of getting the job offer. During the interview other questions will probably come to mind which you had not anticipated.

When asked whether you have questions, you may indicate that many have been answered thus far, but you have a few additional questions. You should have jotted some questions down as you prepared for your interview. Feel free to refer to that list if you need to at this point. The fact that you have given thought to this aspect of the interview and have come prepared will be viewed as a positive by the interviewer. You may have ques-

> *You should have at least two or three questions to ask near the end of the interview.*

tions, for example, about the relationship of this job to other significant functional areas in the company; staff development; training programs; career advancement opportunities; the extent to which promotions are from within the organization; how employee performance is evaluated; or the expected growth of the company. You may want to ask questions that probe areas that were touched on earlier during the interview. For example, if the interviewer has mentioned that the company has an excellent training program, you may have specific questions: What kinds of training would you be offered? How frequently? How long do most training programs last?

If you are still interested in this job, be sure to close the interview by summarizing the strong points you would bring to the position and indicate your continued interest in the job and the company. Ask what the next step will be and when they expect to make a decision. Follow the advice in the next chapter on closing and following up the interview. If you follow this process from beginning to end with intelligent answers and questions, you'll go a long way to getting the job offer despite your not-so-hot background!

Ask Yourself

1. Which job interview questions do I feel most uncomfortable answering?

2. Why would someone want to hire me?

3. How can I best answer this initial question: "*Tell me about yourself.*"

4. What are my three greatest strengths that I would bring to the workplace?

5. Which red flag questions might I be asked based upon reviewing my resume and/or application?

6. What is the best way to answer each of those potential knock-out questions?

7. What questions should I ask the interviewer?

10

Close and Follow Up the Interview

THE INTERVIEW IS NEARLY over. You think it went pretty well. But don't relax yet. It's not over until you get the job offer. So you still have work to do get the job offer.

Sometimes a job offer may be made near the end of the interview, but more often there are other applicants to be interviewed and a hiring decision will be made later. Either way, stay alert and be an active player in bringing the interview to a close.

Respond to a Job Offer

Occasionally the interviewee is offered the job right on the spot. This may happen if you have made a particularly good impression, if it is a hard position to fill, or if the employer needs to fill it fast. Even if you think you want the job, it is usually a good idea to ask for a period of time - at least a day or two - to consider the offer.

There are several reasons why you should do this. First, give yourself time to weigh the advantages and disadvantages of the position. The job which seemed good, as described by the interviewer, may seem less so after you've had the chance to think about it. If you've been a job hopper, make sure this position is right for you. It's time you stay with an organization for a long enough time to break the job hopper cycle.

This advice is also important if you have been sent to the interview through an employment agency. In this case, if you accept and later change your mind and turn down the position, you may be liable for the fee. Even if it is a "fee paid" position - paid by the employer - you are still likely to be held responsible for paying the fee if you accept the position but never actually go to work or work less than a specified period of time - often six months to a year. These regulations vary by state as well as by employment agency, but be especially careful about accepting a job you are uncertain about.

A second reason to ask for time to consider the job offer is to give yourself a chance to check with any other employers with whom you have interviewed, but not yet heard from as to whether they have selected another applicant or are still in the process of making a decision. It is usually acceptable to call a firm where you have been told you are under consideration and tell them you have a job offer, but are interested in where you stand with them. It may speed up their decision and give you two offers from which to compare and choose.

Close With No Job Offer . . . Yet

More often than not, a job offer will not be made at the end of your first interview. For upper level positions the interview process usually consists of several interviews with each applicant under serious consideration. For entry-level positions there are usually several applicants to be interviewed before a decision is made. So don't be disappointed or think you don't have a chance at the job if no offer is made at the close of the interview. However, how you handle the situation is important.

> *Don't be disappointed if no offer is made at the close of the interview. It may take some time before the employer makes a hiring decision.*

The interviewer is likely to verbalize some variation of:

> *"Glad you could come by today. I have enjoyed talking with you. We have several other people to interview. We will be in touch."*

In response, most interviewees shake hands, thank the interviewer, and leave. Don't do this! At this point, try to briefly summarize your strengths as they relate to the job and indicate your continued interest in the job. For example:

> *"I am really glad I had the chance to talk to you. I know the work I did in the stock department at ABC Corporation has parallels to the work you have described here. I think there is a really good 'fit' between my skills and experience and the opening in your company, and I am very interested in the job."*

Or in a different situation:

> *"I am really glad I had the chance to talk with you. I know with what I learned when I reorganized the accounting department at XYZ Corporation, I could increase your profits too. I'm very interested in this job and would look forward to joining your team."*

In addition, ask the interviewer when he or she expects to make the hiring decision. If the response is:

"Friday of next week."

Then ask:

"If I haven't heard from you by the following Monday, may I give you a call?"

Almost everyone will say you may, and you will have solved your problem of wondering when you will hear about the final decision and what to do next. If you have not heard anything by the time the designated Monday arrives, do call. Some interviewers use this technique to see if you will follow through with a call - others are just inconsiderate. By placing the call, if a hiring decision has not yet been made, you will remind the employer of your interest and demonstrate your follow-through. If another applicant has been hired for the job, it is good that you find that out as well so that you can move on to other employers and other job openings.

Send a Thank You Letter

One of the most important things you can do as part of the follow-up process is to send a nice thank you letter in which you:

- Genuinely express your appreciation for the opportunity to interview for the position.

- Repeat your continuing interest in the position and company in reference to your skills.

- Mention that you will call the employer in a few days to inquire about your status.

Here's an example of these three elements in a post-interview thank you letter:

I wish to thank you again for the opportunity to interview for the inventory control position. I enjoyed talking with you and learning more about the work of North Grove Supply.

I remain very interested in this position, especially given your plans to use the new EndPoint Inventory Control System. I'm very familiar with this software program which should save 25 percent in personnel costs within the first year.

I will call you in a few days to see whether you have any further questions and to see how your selection process is progressing. I look forward to hearing from you and hope I will have the opportunity to join your team.

Such a letter will make a positive impression on the employer who seldom receives thoughtful thank you letters from candidates. This letter achieves three important outcomes:

1. The employer remembers you in a positive light - you are a thoughtful person for sending a thank you letter.

2. You let the employer know you really want the job - an often forgotten but important consideration for employers who are not sure if a candidate is highly motivated to take the job. They want employees who really want to work with them.

3. You open the door for making a follow-up call, which may give you another opportunity to sell yourself for the job at a critical decision-making time.

Ask Yourself

1. How can I best close the interview?

2. What should I include in my thank you letter?

3. When should I expect to receive a job offer?

11

When You Need Help Along the Way

W HILE YOU CAN LEARN a lot about conducting an effective job search by reading this and other books, we also know that many people can benefit greatly by seeking the help of others. Indeed, few people are self-starters who can read a book and implement it successfully. Some need assistance with each step in the job search process whereas others need help with only certain critical steps in the process.

Alternative Career Services

You'll find at least 12 alternative career planning and employment services. A few are free, but most charge fees. Each has certain advantages and disadvantages. Approach them with caution. Never sign a contract before you read the fine print, get a second opinion, and talk to former clients about the results they achieved through the service. With these words of caution, let's take a look at the variety of services available.

1. **Public employment services**

    Public employment services usually consist of a state agency which provides employment assistance as well as dispenses unemployment compensation benefits. Employment assistance largely consists of job listings and counseling services. Most employers still do not list with this service, especially for positions paying more than $40,000 a year. Many of these offices are literally "reinventing" themselves for today's new job market with Career One-Stop Centers (www.careeronest op.org), computerized job banks, and other innovative approaches. Many offer useful job services, including self-assessment and job search workshops as well as access to Internet job listings. They also disproportionately work with individuals with not-so-hot backgrounds - ex-offenders, chronically unemployed, and low education and skill levels. Most are linked to America's Job Bank (www.ajb.org), an electronic job board which includes job listings throughout the U.S. and abroad, as well as the U.S. Department of Labor's two websites - America's Career InfoNet (www.acinet.org) and America's Service Locator (www.servicelocator.org). Veterans will find many of the jobs listed through these offices give veterans preference in hiring. You may discover this is your most important resource for professional assistance. Go see for yourself if your state employment office can help you with your job search. If you have Internet access, start by exploring the many local services available through America's Service Locator: www.servicelocator.org.

Just enter your zip code, how far you are willing to travel for a service, and the type of service you desire, and America's Service Locator will indicate where you can find a Career One-Stop Center. This website also identifies a wealth of other career services available to anyone in search of assistance. If you don't have Internet access, call their toll-free number for direct assistance: 1-877-US-2JOBS.

2. Private employment agencies

Private employment agencies work for money, either from applicants or employers. Approximately 8,000 such agencies operate nationwide. Many are highly specialized in technical, scientific, and financial fields. The majority serve the interests of employers. While employers normally pay the placement fee, many agencies charge applicants 10 to 15 percent of their first year salary. These firms have one major advantage: job leads which you may have difficulty uncovering elsewhere. The major disadvantages are that they can be costly and the quality of the firms varies. Make sure you understand the fee structure and what they will do for you before you sign anything.

3. Temporary employment firms

Temporary employment firms offer a variety of employment services to both applicants and employers who are either looking for temporary work and workers or who want to better screen applicants and employers. Many of these firms, such as Labor Finders (www.laborfinders.com), Manpower (www.manpower.com), Olsten (olsten.com), and Kelly Services (kellyservices.com), recruit individuals for a wide range of positions and skill levels as well as full-time employment. Some firms specialize in certain types of workers, such as construction, clerical, IT, and computer personnel. If you are interested in "testing the job waters," you may want to contact these firms. Employers pay for these services. While most firms are listed in the community Yellow Pages, many also operate websites. The following websites are especially popular with individuals interested in part-time, temporary, or contract work: net-temps.com, www.rhii.com, ework.com, emoonlighter.com, aquent.com, dice.com, parttimejobstore.com, talentmarket.monster.com, and talentgateway.com.

4. **College/university placement offices**

College and university placement offices provide in-house career planning services for graduating students. While some assist alumni, don't expect too much help if you have already graduated; contact the alumni office, which may offer employment services. Many college placement offices are understaffed or provide only rudimentary services, such as maintaining a career planning library, coordinating on-campus interviews for graduating seniors, and conducting workshops on how to write resumes and handle interviews. Others provide a full range of well supported services including testing and one-on-one counseling. Many community colleges also offer such services to members of the community on a walk-in basis. You can use their libraries and computerized career assessment programs, take personality and interest inventories, or attend special workshops or full-semester career planning courses which will take you through each step of the career planning and job search processes. Check with your local campus to see what services you might use. Many of the college and university placement offices belong to the National Association of Colleges and Employers (NACE), which operates its own employment website: www.jobweb.com. This site includes a wealth of information on employment for college graduates. Its "Career Library" section provides direct links to hundreds of college and university placement offices: www.jobweb.com/Career Development/collegeres.htm. To find college alumni offices, visit the following websites: alumni.net and www.bcharrispub.com.

5. **Private career and job search firms**

   Private career and job search firms help individuals acquire job search skills and coach them through the process of finding a job. They do not find you a job. Expect to pay anywhere from $1,500 to $10,000 for this service. If you need a structured environment for conducting your job search, contact these firms for assistance. One of the oldest such firms is Bernard Haldane Associates (jobhunting.com and bernardhaldane.com). Many of their pioneering career planning and job search methods are incorporated in this book as well as can be found in five other key job search books: *Haldane's Best Resumes for Professionals, Haldane's Best Cover Letters for Professionals, Haldane's Best Answers to Tough Interview Questions, Haldane's Best Salary Tips for Professionals*, and *Haldane's Best Employment Websites for Professionals*. This firm has over 90 branches located in the U.S., Canada, Australia, and the United Kingdom. Other firms offering related services include Right Management Associates (right.com) and R. L. Stevens & Associates (interviewing.com), and Lee Hecht Harrison (lhh.com/us).

6. **Executive search firms and headhunters**

   Executive search firms work for employers in finding employees to fill critical positions in the $50,000+ salary range. They also are called "headhunters," "management consultants," and "executive recruiters." Don't expect to contract for these services. Executive recruiters work for employers, not applicants. On the other hand, you may want to contact firms that specialize in recruiting individuals with your skill specialty. For a comprehensive listing of these firms, see the latest annual edition of *The Directory of Executive Recruiters* (Kennedy Information, <u>kennedyinfo.com</u>). Several companies, such as <u>resumezapper.com</u>, <u>blastmyresume.com</u>, and <u>resumeblaster.com</u>, offer email resume blasting services that primarily target executive recruiters. Since we have serious doubts about their effectiveness, we caution you to approach these services with a sense of healthy skepticism.

7. **Marketing services**

   Marketing services represent an interesting combination of job search and executive search activities. They can cost $2,500 or more, and they work with individuals anticipating a starting salary of at least $75,000 but preferably over $100,000. A typical operation begins with a client paying a $150 fee for developing psychological, skills, and interests profiles. A marketing plan is outlined and a contract signed for specific services. The firm normally develops a slick "professional" resume and sends it by mail or email, along with a cover letter, to hundreds - maybe thousands - of firms. Clients are then briefed and sent to interviews. Again, approach these services with caution and with the knowledge that you can probably do just as well - if not better - on your own by following the step-by-step advice of this and other job search books.

8. **Women's centers and special career services**

   Women's centers and special career services for displaced workers, such as 40-Plus Clubs (<u>40plus.org/chapters</u>) and Five O'Clock Clubs (<u>fiveoclockclub.com</u>), have been established to respond to the employment needs of special groups. Women's centers are particularly active in sponsoring career planning workshops and job information networks. Special career services arise at times for different categories of employees. For example, unemployed aerospace engineers, teachers, veterans, air traffic controllers, and government employees have formed special groups for developing job search skills and sharing job leads.

9. **Testing and assessment centers**

Testing and assessment centers provide assistance for identifying vocational skills, interests, and objectives. Usually staffed by trained professionals, these centers administer several types of tests and charge from $300 to $800 per person. If you use such services, make sure you are given one or both of the two most popular and reliable tests: *Myers-Briggs Type Indicator®* and the *Strong Interest Inventory®*. You should find both tests helpful in better understanding your interests and decision-making styles. The career office at your local community college or women's center may administer these tests at minimum cost. At the same time, many of these testing and assessment services are now available online.

10. **Job fairs and career conferences**

Job fairs and career conferences are organized by a variety of groups - from schools and government agencies to executive recruiters, employment agencies, and professional associations - to link applicants to employers. Held over one to two days in a hotel or conference center, employers give presentations on their companies, applicants circulate resumes, and employers interview candidates. Many such conferences are organized to attract hard-to-recruit groups, such as engineers, computer programmers, and clerical and service workers.

Several job fairs also are organized for hard-to-place job seekers - ex-offenders, unemployed, people with disabilities, and welfare recipients. These are excellent sources for job leads and information on specific employers - if you are invited to attend or if the meeting is open to the public. Employers pay for this service, although some job fairs or career conferences may charge job seekers a nominal registration fee.

11. Professional associations

Professional associations often provide placement assistance. This usually consists of listing job vacancies in publications, maintaining a resume database, and organizing a job information exchange at annual conferences. Many large associations operate their own online employment sites; members can include their resume in an electronic database and employers can access the database to search for qualified candidates. Annual conferences are good sources for making job contacts in different geographic locations within a particular professional field. But don't expect too much. Talking to people (networking) at professional conferences may yield better results than reading job listings, placing your resume in a database, or interviewing at conference placement centers. For excellent online directories of professional associations, be sure to visit these sites: ipl.org/div/aon and www.asaenet.org.

12. Professional resume writers

Professional resume writers are increasingly playing an important role in career planning. Each year thousands of job seekers rely on these professionals for assistance in writing their resumes. Many of them also provide useful job search tips on resume distribution, cover letters, and networking. Charging from $100 to $500 for writing a resume, they work with the whole spectrum of job seekers - entry-level to senior executives making millions of dollars each year. While not certified career counselors, many of these professionals have their own associations and certification groups. If you are interested in using a professional resume writer, visit these websites for information on this network of career professionals: www.parw.com, prwra.com, and nrwa.com.

Locating a Certified Career Professional

Certified career professionals have their own associations. If you are interested in contacting one for assistance, we advise you to first visit these websites for locating a career professional:

- **National Board for Certified Counselors, Inc.**   nbcc.org
- **National Career Development Association**   ncda.org
- **Certified Career Coaches**   certifiedcareercoaches.com
- **Career Planning and Adult Development Network**   careernetwork.org

Dealing With Difficult Backgrounds

If, as we noted throughout this book, you have a difficult or not-so-hot background that requires special intervention - from counseling to therapy - by all means seek professional assistance. While the tips and strategies outlined in this book should prove very useful, you may need additional assistance that goes beyond the scope of this book. Individuals with backgrounds involving incarceration, drug and alcohol abuse, mental illness, and learning disabilities may find assistance through local social service departments, Workforce Development Programs, hospitals, YMCAs, YWCAs, churches, and other local nonprofit groups (Goodwill Industries, Project RIO, Welcome Home Ministries) experienced in working with such individuals. In Baltimore, Maryland, for example, over

80 nonprofit organizations belong to a network of organizations that assists ex-offenders in finding employment. We also publish a unique catalog of nearly 300 career-related resources relevant to individuals with difficult but promising backgrounds. You can download a copy of this catalog, as well as several other catalogs, from the home page of the publisher's website:

www.impactpublications.com

Useful Books and Websites

Numerous books and websites are available to help job seekers improve their interview skills.

Books on Job Interviewing

- *101 Dynamite Questions to Ask at Your Job Interview* (Richard Fein)
- *101 Great Answers to the Toughest Interview Questions* (Ron Fry)
- *250 Job Interview Questions You'll Most Likely Be Asked* (Peter Veruki)
- *Adams Job Interview Almanac, with CD-ROM* (Adams Media)
- *Haldane's Best Answers to Tough Interview Questions* (Bernard Haldane Associates)
- *Interview for Success* (Caryl and Ron Krannich)
- *Interview Rehearsal Book* (Deb Gottesman and Buzz Mauro)
- *Job Interviews for Dummies* (Joyce Lain Kennedy)
- *KeyWords to Nail Your Job Interview* (Wendy S. Enelow)
- *Nail the Job Interview* (Caryl and Ron Krannich)
- *Naked at the Interview* (Burton Jay Nadler)
- *The Perfect Interview* (John Drake)
- *Power Interviews* (Neil M. Yeager and Lee Hough)
- *Preparing for the Behavior-Based Interview* (Terry L. Fitzwater)

- *Savvy Interviewing: The Nonverbal Advantage*
  (Caryl and Ron Krannich)
- *Sweaty Palms* (H. Anthony Medley)

Interview-Related Websites

- **Monster.com**   http://interview.monster.com and
                                 http://content.monster.com/
                                 jobinfo/interview
- **InterviewPro**   interviewpro.com
- **JobInterview.net**   job-interview.net
- **Interview Coach**   interviewcoach.com
- **Quintessential Careers** quintcareers.com/intvres.html
- **Riley Guide**   rileyguide.com/netintv.html
- **WinningTheJob**   winningthejob.com

Several additional books and websites focus on salary negotiations - which should occur after receiving a job offer, either at the very end of the interview or in a separate interview session:

Books on Salary Negotiations

- *101 Salary Secrets* (Daniel Porot)
- *Are You Paid What You're Worth?* (Michael F. O'Malley and Suzanne Oaks)
- *Better Than Money* (David E. Gumpert)
- *Dynamite Salary Negotiations* (Ron and Caryl Krannich)
- *Get More Money On Your Next Job* (Lee E. Miller)
- *Get Paid What You're Worth* (Robin Pinkley and Gregory Northcraft)
- *Get a Raise in 7 Days* (Ron and Caryl Krannich)
- *Haldane's Best Salary Tips for Professionals* (Bernard Haldane Associates)
- *Interviewing and Salary Negotiation* (Kate Wendleton)
- *Negotiating Your Salary* (Jack Chapman)

Salary-Related Websites

- Salary.com — salary.com
- JobStar.org — jobstar.org
- Wageweb — www.wageweb.com
- Abbott-Langer — abbott-langer.com
- Robert Half International — www.rhii.com
- Monster.com — http://salary.monster.com and http://content.salary.monster.com
- SalarySource.com — salarysource.com
- Quintessential Careers — quintcareers.com/salary_negotiation.html
- Riley Guide — rileyguide.com/netintv.html
- WinningTheJob — winningthejob.com
- SalaryExpert — salaryexpert.com

Ask Yourself

1. What type of career assistance could I use?

2. Which services are available in my community?

3. Which of the 12 alternative career services might best meet
my needs?

4. What additional books and websites should I explore?

Index

A

Accomplishments:
  questions about, 52-53
  talking about, 82
Achievements (see Accomplishments)
Alcohol abuse, 109-111
Answers:
  evasive, 80
  honest, 33
  incomplete, 78
  practicing, 86
Appearance, 27-28, 57-59, 77
Applications:
  completing, 48-49
  inaccurate, 2
Arrival, 64-66, 76, 81
Assessment centers, 126
Attitudes:
  bad, 77
  changing, xi

B

Background:
  checks, 2
  explaining, 69
  not-so-hot, x, 13-21
Backgrounds, 2
Bad-mouthing, 80
Behavior:
  assessing, 34
  changing, xii, 34-38, 43
  excuses for, 76
  high-risk firing, 14-16
  inappropriate interview, 77
  nonverbal, 56-57
  predicting, 5, 14, 16
Believability, 27

Benefits, 82
Body language, 26, 29, 59-61

C

Candidates, ix, 1
Career:
  conferences, 126-127
  professionals, 128
  resources, 129-131
  services, 121-128
Character, 1
Characteristics, 4-5
Closing, 84, 114-119
Clues:
  nonverbal, 26-27
  red flag, 14, 39
  verbal, 25-27
Coherence, 77
College career centers, 123-124
Communication:
  nonverbal, 26-27, 56-57, 62-63
  verbal, 25-27, 56, 62
Confidence, 79
Cooperation, 6-7
Criminal record (see
  Ex-offenders)

D

Deception, 79
Degree (see Education)
Dependability, 5-6
Diploma (see Education)
Direction, 78
Disrespectful, 81
Dress:
  importance of, 27-28
  men, 57-58
  women, 58-59

Drug abuse, 109-111

E
Education, 17-18, 52, 97-98
Employee:
    behavior, 5-11
    desirable, 1, 4-5
    trustworthy, 9
    turnover, 9-10
Employers:
    conning, 4, 12
    expectations of, 24-25
    goals, 75
    thinking like, xii
    wants of, 1-11
Employment services
    college, 123-134
    private, 122
    public, 121-122
    temporary, 122-123
Enthusiasm, 29, 78
Examples:
    honest, 33
    job search, ix
    providing, 92
Excuses, 76
Executive search, 125
Ex-offenders, 20, 105-109
Experience:
    lacking, 17
    questions about, 52, 94-95
Explanations, 39-44
Eye contact, 28, 61, 80

F
Facial expression, 28-29, 61-62
Fidgeting, 60
Fired:
    being, 18, 39
    questions about being, 98-99
    why, 39-41
Focus, 19, 77
Follow up, 114-119
Following orders, 7-8
Friends, 66

G
Gestures, 26, 28, 61
Goals, 53
Grades, 17, 95-97

Greed, 82
Grooming:
    men, 57-58
    women, 58-59

H
Handshake, 49-50, 80
Health, 78
Hiring:
    clues, 14, 24-31
    mistakes, 4, 11
    problems, 4, 13, 14
    red flags, 14-22
    risks, 16
    smarter, 5
Honesty, 79

I
Impressions, 75, 76
Information, 70
Initiative, 78-79
Intelligence, 83
Interest, 30, 80
Interview(s):
    arriving at, 64-66
    beginning, 68
    closing, 81, 84
    errors, 74-84
    invitation to, 74
    multiple, 3
    practicing, 54
    site, 65-66
    thank you, 117-118

J
Job:
    assistance, 120-131
    fairs, 126-127
    fit, 69
    focus, 19, 102-103
    hopper, 18-19
    hopping, 9-11, 100-102
    offer, 114-117
    services, 120-128
Jokes, 81

K
Knock-outs:
    identifying, 21-23
    types of, 14-16

L

Language, 77
Letters:
    follow-up, 117-118
    sending, 117
Listening:
    instructions, 8-9
    interview, 68-69
    skills, 83
Lying, 106

M

Marketing services, 125-126
Memorizing, 48, 51, 85
Men, 57-58
Messages, 27, 29-30, 69-71
Motivation, xi, 5, 20, 30, 53

N

Names, 67
Needy, 82
Nervousness, 28, 79
Nonverbal (see Communication)

O

Objections, 33, 94-111
Orders, 7-8
Over-qualified, 20-21, 110-111

P

Parking, 66
Performance, 1, 14
Personal questions, 51
Plans, 54
Practice, 54, 65
Preparation, 32-55, 65, 83-84
Professional associations, 127

Q

Qualifications, 20-21
Questions:
    accomplishments, 52-53
    anticipating, 50-51
    asking, 111-112
    behavior-based, 3, 8, 93-94
    closing, 116-117
    difficult background, 71
    education, 52, 88-89, 97-98
    experience, 89-90, 94-95
    fired, 98-99

future, 54
goals, 53, 90
job focus, 102-103
job hopper, 100-102
job-related, 91
likely, 86-91
motivation, 53, 87-88
personal life, 51
personality, 87-88
predicting, 85
red flag, 94-111
references, 103-105
resume-related, 92
review, 11-12, 22-23, 30-31, 55,
    73, 112-113, 119, 131
situation-based, 93-94
skills, 89-90
training, 88-89
unexpected, 91-93
wacky, 91-93
what if, 3
work style, 52-53

R

Reception area, 67-68, 76
Receptionist, 67
Red flags:
    addressing, 38
    changing, 37-38
    examples of, 13-23
    explaining, 38-39
    identifying, 33-37
    lowering, 39-42
    raising, 70
    talking about, 71-72
    volunteering, 44
References:
    contacting, 49
    giving, 20
    poor, 19-20
    questions about, 103-104
    selecting, 49
    strongest, 49
Remembered, 72
Research:
    conducting, 46
    online, 47
Responses, 51
Responsibility, 23, 38, 41, 107, 109
Resume writers, 127-128

Resumes:
  inaccurate, 2
  writing, 127-128

S
Salary:
  resources, 130-131
  talking about, 81
Scent, 28, 57, 59, 78
Screening, 1
Shoulders, 29, 50
Sitting, 60
Skills:
  interpersonal, 6-7
  workplace, 4-5
Stories, 15, 106
Stress, 75
Success, ix, 3-4

T
Talking:
  briefly, 71
  too much, 41, 71, 81
Tests, 3
Trustworthiness, 9, 75
Truthfulness, xi, 1, 3-4, 9, 11, 27, 43
Turnover, 9-11

V
Value, 1
Vocal Expression, 62
Voice, 27, 28

W
Waiting, 67
Women, 58-59
Women's centers, 126
Work:
  habits, 5-6
  history, 92
Work style, 52-53
Workplace characteristics, 4-5

The Authors

F OR MORE THAN TWO DECADES Ron and Caryl Krannich, Ph.Ds, have pursued a passion – assisting hundreds of thousands of individuals, from students, the unemployed, and ex-offenders to military personnel, international job seekers, and CEOs, in making critical job and career transitions. Focusing on key job search skills, career changes, and employment fields, their impressive body of work has helped shape career thinking and behavior both in the United States and abroad. Their sound advice has changed numerous lives, including their own!

Ron and Caryl are two of America's leading career and travel writers who have authored, co-authored, or ghost-written more than 70 books. A former Peace Corps Volunteer and Fulbright Scholar, Ron received his Ph.D. in Political Science from Northern Illinois University. Caryl received her Ph.D. in Speech Communication from Penn State University. Together they operate Development Concepts Incorporated, a training, consulting, and publishing firm in Virginia.

The Krannichs are both former university professors, high school teachers, management trainers, and consultants. As trainers and consultants, they have completed numerous projects on management, career development, local government, population planning, and rural development in the United States and abroad. Their career books focus on key job search skills, military and civilian career transitions, government and international careers, travel jobs, and nonprofit organizations and include such classics as *High Impact Resumes and Letters, Interview for Success*, and *Change Your Job, Change Your Life*. Their books represent one of today's most comprehensive collections of career writing. With over 2 million copies in print, their publications are widely available in bookstores, libraries, and career centers. No strangers to the Internet world, they have written *America's Top Internet Job Sites* and *The Directory of Websites for International Jobs* and published several Internet recruitment and job search books. They also have developed career-related websites: impactpublications.com, winningthejob.com, contentforcareers.com, and veteransworld.com. Many of their career tips appear on such major websites as monster.com, careerbuilder.com, employmentguide.com, and campuscareercenter.com.

Ron and Caryl live a double life with travel being their best kept *"do what you love"* career secret. Authors of over 20 travel-shopping guidebooks on various destinations around the world, they continue to pursue their international and travel interests through their innovative *Treasures and Pleasures of...Best of the Best* travel-shopping series and related websites: ishoparoundtheworld.com, contentfor travel.com, and travel-smarter.com. When not found at their home and business in Virginia, they are probably somewhere in Europe, Asia, Africa, the Middle East, the South Pacific, the Caribbean, or the Americas following their other passion – researching and writing about quality antiques, arts, crafts, jewelry, hotels, and restaurants as well as adhering to the career advice they give to others: *"Pursue a passion that enables you to do what you really love to do."*

As both career and travel experts, the Krannichs' work is frequently featured in major newspapers, magazines, and newsletters as well as on radio, television, and the Internet. Available for interviews, consultation, and presentations, they can be contacted as follows:

Ron and Caryl Krannich
krannich@impactpublications.com

Career Resources

T HE FOLLOWING CAREER RESOURCES are available directly from Impact Publications. Full descriptions of each title as well as nine downloadable catalogs, videos, and software can be found on our website: www.impact publications.com. Complete the following form or list the titles, include shipping (see formula at the end), enclose payment, and send your order to:

IMPACT PUBLICATIONS
9104 Manassas Drive, Suite N
Manassas Park, VA 20111-5211 USA
1-800-361-1055 (orders only)
Tel. 703-361-7300 or Fax 703-335-9486
Email address: info@impactpublications.com
Quick & easy online ordering: www.impactpublications.com

Orders from individuals must be prepaid by check, money order, or major credit card. We accept telephone, fax, and email orders.

Qty.	TITLES	Price	TOTAL
Featured Title			
____	Job Interview Tips for People With Not-So-Hot Backgrounds	$14.95	_____
Companion Titles By Authors			
____	America's Top 100 Jobs for People Without a Four Your Degree	$19.95	_____
____	America's Top Internet Job Sites	$19.95	_____
____	Change Your Job, Change Your Life	$21.95	_____
____	Discover the Best Jobs for You	$15.95	_____
____	Dynamite Salary Negotiations	$15.95	_____
____	I Want to Do Something Else, But I'm Not Sure What It Is	$15.95	_____
____	Interview for Success	$15.95	_____

____ The Job Hunting Guide	14.95	_____
____ Nail the Job Interview	13.95	_____
____ No One Will Hire Me!	13.95	_____
____ Savvy Interviewing: The Nonverbal Advantage	12.95	_____
____ The Savvy Networker	13.95	_____

Changing Addictive and Not-So-Hot Behaviors

____ Angry Men	14.95	_____
____ Angry Women	14.95	_____
____ Denial Is Not a River in Egypt	11.95	_____
____ If Life Is a Game, These Are the Rules	15.00	_____
____ If Success Is a Game, These Are the Rules	17.50	_____
____ No One Is Unemployable	29.95	_____
____ No One Will Hire Me!	13.95	_____
____ Passages Through Recovery	14.00	_____
____ Sex, Drugs, Gambling and Chocolate	15.95	_____
____ Stop the Chaos	12.95	_____
____ The Truth About Addiction and Recovery	14.00	_____
____ Understanding the Twelve Steps	12.00	_____
____ You Can Heal Your Life	17.95	_____

Attitude and Motivation

____ 100 Ways to Motivate Yourself	18.99	_____
____ Change Your Attitude	15.99	_____
____ Reinventing Yourself	18.99	_____

Inspiration and Empowerment

____ 101 Secrets of Highly Effective Speakers	15.95	_____
____ Do What You Love for the Rest of Your Life	24.95	_____
____ Dream It Do It	16.95	_____
____ Life Strategies	13.95	_____
____ Power of Purpose	20.00	_____
____ Practical Dreamer's Handbook	13.95	_____
____ Self Matters	14.00	_____
____ Seven Habits of Highly Effective People	14.00	_____
____ Who Moved My Cheese?	19.95	_____

Testing and Assessment

____ Career Tests	12.95	_____
____ Discover the Best Jobs for You	15.95	_____
____ Discover What You're Best At	14.00	_____
____ Do What You Are	18.95	_____
____ Finding Your Perfect Work	16.95	_____
____ I Could Do Anything If Only I Knew What It Was	13.95	_____
____ I Want to Do Something Else, But I'm Not Sure What It Is	15.95	_____
____ Now, Discover Your Strengths	27.00	_____
____ Pathfinder	14.00	_____
____ What Should I Do With My Life?	24.95	_____
____ What Type Am I?	14.95	_____
____ What's Your Type of Career?	17.95	_____

Career Exploration and Job Strategies

____	5 Patterns of Extraordinary Careers	17.95 _____
____	25 Jobs That Have It All	12.95 _____
____	50 Cutting Edge Jobs	15.95 _____
____	95 Mistakes Job Seekers Make and	
	How to Avoid Them	13.95 _____
____	100 Great Jobs and How to Get Them	17.95 _____
____	101 Ways to Recession-Proof Your Career	14.95 _____
____	America's Top 100 Jobs for People	
	Without a Four-Year Degree	19.95 _____
____	Best Jobs for the 21st Century	19.95 _____
____	Career Change	14.95 _____
____	Career Intelligence	15.95 _____
____	Change Your Job, Change Your Life	
	(9th Edition)	21.95 _____
____	Cool Careers for Dummies	19.99 _____
____	Directory of Executive Recruiters	49.95 _____
____	Five Secrets to Finding a Job	12.95 _____
____	Haldane's Best Secrets of the	
	Hidden Job Market	15.95 _____
____	High-Tech Careers for Low-Tech People	14.95 _____
____	How to Get a Job and Keep It	16.95 _____
____	How to Succeed Without a Career Path	13.95 _____
____	Job Hunting Guide: Transitioning	
	From College to Career	14.95 _____
____	Knock 'Em Dead	14.95 _____
____	Me, Myself, and I, Inc.	17.95 _____
____	Occupational Outlook Handbook	18.95 _____
____	O*NET Dictionary of Occupational Titles	39.95 _____
____	Quit Your Job and Grow Some Hair	15.95 _____
____	Rites of Passage at $100,000 to $1 Million+	29.95 _____
____	What Color Is Your Parachute?	17.95 _____
____	Working Identify	26.95 _____

Internet Job Search

____	100 Top Internet Job Sites	12.95 _____
____	America's Top Internet Job Sites	19.95 _____
____	CareerXroads (annual)	26.95 _____
____	Career Exploration On the Internet	24.95 _____
____	Cyberspace Job Search Kit	18.95 _____
____	Directory of Websites for International Jobs	19.95 _____
____	Guide to Internet Job Searching	14.95 _____
____	Haldane's Best Employment Websites	
	for Professionals	15.95 _____
____	Job Search Online for Dummies	
	(with CD-ROM)	24.99 _____

Resumes and Letters

____	101 Great Tips for a Dynamite Resume	13.95 _____
____	175 Best Cover Letters	14.95 _____

____ 201 Dynamite Job Search Letters	19.95	_____
____ America's Top Resumes for America's Top Jobs	19.95	_____
____ Best KeyWords for Resumes, Cover Letters, & Interviews	17.95	_____
____ Best Resumes and CVs for International Jobs	24.95	_____
____ Best Resumes for $100,000+ Jobs	24.95	_____
____ Best Resumes for People Without a Four-Year Degree	19.95	_____
____ Best Cover Letters for $100,000+ Jobs	24.95	_____
____ Cover Letters for Dummies	16.99	_____
____ Cover Letters That Knock 'Em Dead	12.95	_____
____ Cyberspace Resume Kit	18.95	_____
____ Dynamite Cover Letters	14.95	_____
____ Dynamite Resumes	14.95	_____
____ e-Resumes	14.95	_____
____ Gallery of Best Cover Letters	18.95	_____
____ Gallery of Best Resumes	18.95	_____
____ Haldane's Best Cover Letters for Professionals	15.95	_____
____ Haldane's Best Resumes for Professionals	15.95	_____
____ High Impact Resumes and Letters	19.95	_____
____ Resume Shortcuts	14.95	_____
____ Resumes for Dummies	16.99	_____
____ Resumes for the Health Care Professional	14.95	_____
____ Resumes in Cyberspace	14.95	_____
____ Resumes That Knock 'Em Dead	12.95	_____
____ The Savvy Resume Writer	12.95	_____
____ Sure-Hire Resumes	14.95	_____

Networking

____ Dynamite Telesearch	12.95	_____
____ A Foot in the Door	14.95	_____
____ Golden Rule of Schmoozing	12.95	_____
____ Great Connections	11.95	_____
____ How to Work a Room	14.00	_____
____ Masters of Networking	16.95	_____
____ Power Networking	14.95	_____
____ The Savvy Networker	13.95	_____

Dress, Image, and Etiquette

____ Dressing Smart for Men	16.95	_____
____ Dressing Smart for Women	16.95	_____
____ Power Etiquette	14.95	_____
____ Professional Impressions	14.95	_____

Interviews

____ 101 Dynamite Questions to Ask At Your Job Interview	13.95	_____
____ Haldane's Best Answers to Tough Interview Questions	15.95	_____
____ Interview for Success	15.95	_____

___ Job Interview Tips for People With		
Not-So-Hot Backgrounds	14.95	_____
___ Job Interviews for Dummies	16.99	_____
___ KeyWords to Nail Your Job Interview	17.95	_____
___ Nail the Job Interview!	13.95	_____
___ The Savvy Interviewer	10.95	_____

Salary Negotiations

___ Better Than Money	18.95	_____
___ Dynamite Salary Negotiations	15.95	_____
___ Get a Raise in 7 Days	14.95	_____
___ Haldane's Best Salary Tips for Professionals	15.95	_____

Military in Transition

___ Jobs and the Military Spouse	17.95	_____
___ Military Resumes and Cover Letters	21.95	_____

Ex-Offenders in Transition

___ 9 to 5 Beats Ten to Life	15.00	_____
___ 99 Days and a Get Up	9.95	_____
___ Ex-Offender's Job Search Companion	9.95	_____
___ Man, I Need a Job	7.95	_____
___ Putting the Bars Behind You (6 books)	64.70	_____

Government and Nonprofit Jobs

___ Complete Guide to Public Employment	19.95	_____
___ Federal Applications That Get Results	23.95	_____
___ Federal Employment From A to Z	14.50	_____
___ FBI Careers	18.95	_____
___ Find a Federal Job Fast!	15.95	_____
___ Jobs and Careers With Nonprofit Organizations	17.95	_____
___ Ten Steps to a Federal Job	39.95	_____

International and Travel Jobs

___ Back Door Guide to Short-Term Job Adventures	21.95	_____
___ Inside Secrets to Finding a Career in Travel	14.95	_____
___ International Jobs	19.00	_____
___ International Job Finder	19.95	_____
___ Jobs for Travel Lovers	17.95	_____
___ Teaching English Abroad	15.95	_____
___ Work Your Way Around the World	17.95	_____

VIDEOS

Video Series

___ 50 Best Jobs for the 21st Century	545.00	_____
___ 60- Minute Self-Renewal Video Series	1999.95	_____
___ Job Finding for People With Disabilities		
Video Series	199.95	_____
___ Job Search Skills Video Series	799.00	_____
___ Job Success Without a College Degree Series	560.00	_____

____ Managing Your Personal Finances Series	499.00	_____
____ One Stop Career Center Video Series	599.00	_____
____ Portfolio Resumes Series	150.00	_____
____ Quick Job Search Video Series	545.00	_____
____ Road to Re-Employment Video Series	219.95	_____
____ Welfare-to-Work Video Series	545.00	_____
____ Work Maturity Skills Video Series	799.00	_____

Individual Videos

Interview, Networking, and Salary Videos

____ Build a Network for Work and Life	129.00	_____
____ Common Mistakes People Make in Interviews	79.95	_____
____ Exceptional Interviewing Tips	79.00	_____
____ Extraordinary Answers to Interview Questions	79.95	_____
____ Extreme Interview	69.00	_____
____ Make a First Good Impression	129.00	_____
____ Mastering the Interview	98.00	_____
____ Seizing the Job Interview	79.00	_____
____ Quick Interview Video	149.00	_____
____ Quick Salary Negotiations Video	149.00	_____
____ Why Should I Hire You?	129.00	_____

Dress and Image Videos

____ Looking Sharp: Dressing for Success	99.00	_____
____ Looking Sharp: Grooming for Success	99.00	_____
____ Tips and Techniques to Improve Your Total Image	98.00	_____

Resumes, Applications, and Cover Letter Videos

____ The Complete Job Application	129.00	_____
____ Effective Resumes	79.95	_____
____ Ideal Resume	79.95	_____
____ Quick Cover Letter Video	149.00	_____
____ Quick Resume Video	149.00	_____
____ Resumes, Cover Letters, and Portfolios	98.00	_____
____ Ten Commandments of Resumes	79.95	_____
____ Your Resume	99.00	_____

Assessment and Goal Setting Videos

____ Career Path Interest Inventory	149.00	_____
____ Career S.E.L.F. Assessment	89.00	_____
____ Skills Identification	129.00	_____
____ You DO Have Experience	149.00	_____

Attitude, Motivation, and Empowerment Videos

____ Down But Not Out	129.00	_____
____ Gumby Attitude	69.00	_____
____ Know Yourself	109.95	_____
____ Positive Feet	129.00	_____
____ Take This Job and Love It	79.95	_____

Career Exploration Videos

____	Career Exploration and Planning	98.00	_____
____	Great Jobs Without a College Degree	98.00	_____

Job Search Strategies Videos

____	Tough Times Job Strategies	89.95	_____
____	Very Quick Job Search Video	149.00	_____

SOFTWARE

____	Interview Skills for the Future	199.00	_____
____	Job Browser Pro 1.3	359.00	_____
____	Job Search Skills for the 21st Century	199.00	_____
____	Multimedia Career Center	385.00	_____
____	Multimedia Career Pathway	199.00	_____
____	Multimedia Occupational GOE Assessment Program	449.00	_____
____	Multimedia Personal Development CD-ROM Series	450.00	_____
____	OOH Career Center	349.95	_____
____	School-to-Work Career Center	385.95	_____

SUBTOTAL _____

Virginia residents add 4.5% sales tax _____

POSTAGE/HANDLING ($5 for first product and 8% of SUBTOTAL) **$5.00** _____

8% of SUBTOTAL – – – – – – – – – – ⌐⎯⎯⎯⎯⎯⎯⎯⎯⎯⎯⎯⎯

TOTAL ENCLOSED – – – – – – ⌐⎯⎯⎯⎯⎯⎯⎯⎯⎯⎯⎯⎯

SHIP TO:

NAME _____

ADDRESS _____

_____

_____

PAYMENT METHOD:

❏ I enclose check/money order for $ _____ made payable to IMPACT PUBLICATIONS.

❏ Please charge $ _____ to my credit card:

❏ Visa ❏ MasterCard ❏ American Express ❏ Discover

Card # _____ Expiration date: ____/____

Signature _____